STO

ACPL ITEM
DISCARDED

Crisis on the Rio Grande

Crisis on the Rio Grande

Poverty, Unemployment, and Economic Development on the Texas-Mexico Border

Dianne C. Betts
and Daniel J. Slottje
with Jesus Vargas-Garcia

Westview Press

BOULDER • SAN FRANCISCO • OXFORD

Copyright © 1994 by Westview Press, Inc.

Published in 1994 in the United States of America by Westview Press, Inc., 5500 Central Avenue, Boulder, Colorado 80301-2877, and in the United Kingdom by Westview Press, 36 Lonsdale Road, Summertown, Oxford OX2 7EW

Library of Congress Cataloging-in-Publication Data
Betts, Dianne C.
    Crisis on the Rio Grande : poverty, umemployment, and economic
development on the Texas-Mexico border / Dianne C. Betts and Daniel J. Slottje
        p.   cm.
    Includes bibliographical references and index.
    ISBN 0-8133-8812-0
    1. Mexican-American Border Region—Economic conditions.
2. Mexican-American Border Region—Social conditions.   3. Canada,
Treaties, etc.   1992 Oct. 7.   I. Slottje, Daniel Jonathan, 1957– .
II. Title.
HC137.M46847   1994
330.972'1—dc20   93-38472
                                                                                      CIP

Printed and bound in the United States of America

        The paper used in this publication meets the requirements
∞   of the American National Standard for Permanence of Paper
        for Printed Library Materials Z39.48-1984.

10   9   8   7   6   5   4   3   2   1

Contents

Tables and Figures

Figures

Acknowledgments

We are indebted to a number of people and institutions for their help with the research for this study. In particular we owe thanks to the Government Documents staff and the interlibrary loan staff of Fondren Library at Southern Methodist University, the staff of the Economic Research Center for Mexico in Bala Cynwyd, Pennsylvania, the staff of the Bureau of Business Research in Austin, Texas, and the staff of the Texas governor's office. We especially appreciate the support we received from the Region 7 Office of the Texas Department of Human Services and the Coalition of Community Service Agencies. Their personal attention put a human face on the issues of the border.

We have benefitted from the excellent editorial staff at Westview Press as well as the comments from anonymous referees. The Federal Reserve Bank of Dallas and the Texas Agricultural Market Research Center both allowed us to reprint various tables. In any case, the interpretation and any errors this study might contain rest solely with us.

Dianne C. Betts
Daniel J. Slottje

Introduction

Each year, beginning in September, thousands of trailers, mobile homes, and recreational vehicles snake their way through Texas from the Midwest. These snow-to-sun migrants, known as Texas snowbirds, settle for four to eight months in the broad delta that comprises the Lower Rio Grande Valley (LRGV). The Texas portion of this "Magic Valley" is approximately 60 miles deep and 160 miles long.[1] Officially, it includes Cameron, Hidalgo, and Willacy counties. For the purpose of this study, however, Starr county will also be included. On the Mexican side of the Rio Grande River lies the state of Tamaulipas with two large population centers, Matamoros and Reynosa, as well as a number of other smaller towns. It is in this region that the relative prosperity and poverty of the United States and Mexico creates a unique relationship governed by its own set of rules.

The influx of these cold-weather migrants adds to the diversity of a region which is tri-cultural. Mexican-Americans, Anglos, and Mexican Nationals constitute the majority of the more than 1.7 million people living in this combination of rural-agrarian and urban-industrial areas. A constant two-way exchange flows between Mexico and Texas as people shop, work, visit friends and relatives, and seek health care, creating a curious sense of unity and a unique *frontera* ambiance within the "Valley." The palm trees, bougainvillea, and oleanders contrast with the starkness of the coastal plain of southern Texas and the arid lands of northern Mexico.

Amidst this tropical lushness exist a number of major social and economic problems: severe poverty, illegal immigration, overpopulation, and unemployment to name a few. This contrasts sharply with the more traditional images of Texans: the rich and wily oil barons surrounded by opulence as they scheme their way through one international oil deal after another; or the tough, hard-drinking, hard-fighting cowboys who control vast acres of ranch land with an ability and intensity equal to that of the oil barons. "Rich" and "Texan" go together like "ham" and "eggs" in the minds of much of the world. The LRGV, however, comprises another, less attractive Texas -- one marked by many of the characteristics put forward by Michael Harrington in his classic study of poverty: Spanish-speaking, unemployed, and residents of a depressed region.[2] The Texas portion of

1

the border region possesses a level of economic development that bears closer resemblance to the level of development in the Third World than it does to the rest of the United States, particularly in the rural parts of the region. The poverty in the Lower Rio Grande Valley (LRGV) is a direct result of economic and social processes which have worsened over time and created poverty levels without equal in the rest of northern Mexico and the United States. This study attempts to characterize, quantify, and analyze the conditions under which people in this region live and why they live this way.

In 1990, U.S. Census studies listed the population of Cameron, Hidalgo, Starr, and Willacy counties as 701,888. This figure, however, excludes the thousands of "snowbirds" who either own property in the LRGV or live in the numerous trailer parks and guest apartment complexes. Poverty is a fact of life for the majority of the permanent inhabitants of these counties. In most of the towns in these counties, Mexican-American "barrios" exist which differ from similar ethnic neighborhoods in urban areas further north. These barrios are dotted with tiny, single-family dwellings, often several to a small lot. Efforts by city and county officials to condemn them have been unsuccessful. In the countryside, urban barrios are replaced by subdivisions known as *colonias*. Here the poverty is more visibly acute. The frequently unmarked streets are lined with one-room wooden shacks, wooden outhouses, and bright green garden hoses attached to the only source of treated water, a single outdoor spigot. Just as poverty in rural Mississippi or Appalachia lies off the "beaten track," these *colonias*, too, remain relatively invisible since many of them lie far from major highways and roads. One can travel all the way from Brownsville to Rio Grande City on Hwy. 83 and never see them. However, they are gaining increasing visibility as attempts are made to solve the problems plaguing them.

There are several densely populated cities in the LRGV, including Brownsville and Harlingen in Cameron county and McAllen in Hidalgo county with a combined population of 231,718. Economic activity in the Valley revolves around agribusiness, food processing, shipping, oil processing, tourism, fishing, and manufacturing. Much of the area is famous as a winter resort and as a gateway to Mexico. The "snowbirds" that swell the population during the fall and winter months play an important role in tourism, spending more than $50 million each year.[3] Despite this, in 1990 unemployment for the area ranged from 11.7% for Cameron county to 36.1% in Starr county.[4]

On the Mexican side of the border region, the most important urban areas are Matamoros, Reynosa, and Camargo-Rio Bravo with a combined population of 678,941. Tourism, agriculture and services comprise the most important economic activities, but maquiladora plants also play an important role in the region. A large Mexican petrochemical complex is located in Reynosa and employs thousands of people drawn from low-income areas throughout Mexico. In 1990, the unemployment rate in the state of Tamaulipas was 5.0%, significantly lower than the 8.3% national average for Mexico. These cities have experienced high population growth rates over the past two decades, brought about by several factors. First, birth rates in this area have been high. Second, a large migratory flow to these cities from the interior of Mexico has occurred, primarily from rural areas. Since 1970, net immigration to the state of Tamaulipas has been 271,783. This is more than the combined population of the three largest cities on the Texas side of the LRGV.[5]

Such a large demographic change has predictably exacerbated several problems. Irregular settlements with all the negative characteristics of rural poverty have sprung up all along the Mexico-Texas border. These areas have increased in number over time and have been characterized by inadequate housing, and a general lack of health, transportation, and other public services. Part of the problem stems from the introduction of the maquiladora industry into the Mexican border region. While the industrial development associated with these plants helps to ease some of the problems in the region, at the same time it is said to attract yet more immigrants, thereby worsening existing problems within the area. The implementation of a Free Trade Agreement between Mexico and the United States should have a significant impact on the area and help alleviate some of these problems.

Renewed interest in Mexico as a prominent trading partner makes a study of the socio-economic conditions of the border region even more imperative. In this book, we describe a world where hunger, destitution, unemployment, and despair exist. It is the "other Texas" not captured in the media image of oil and the Wild West. We examine the demographic changes that have transpired over the past decade and have contributed to the problems which exist on both sides of the border. We also explore in depth the human tragedy that exists in this area and efforts currently underway to deal with this tragedy. While doing so, we examine the efficacy of public policy that was ostensibly implemented to alleviate these problems. We investigate the role economic development plays (and will continue to play) in easing the conditions which exist on the border by looking at the effect migration patterns and maquiladora plants have had (and will continue to have) in the area. Finally, we consider the impact that a Free Trade Agreement could have on the region and suggest policy recommendations that may help alleviate current border problems and could lead the way in preventing future ones.

4 *Introduction*

Notes

1. T.R. Fehrenbach. *Texas: A Salute from Above.* (San Antonio: World Publishing Services, Inc., 1985), p. 267. The LRGV has been known both as the "Magic Valley" because of its long growing season and as the "Valley of Tears" because of the poverty of many of its inhabitants.

2. M. Harrington. *The Other America: Poverty in the United States.* (New York: Penguin Books, 1981).

3. C.H. Rush, Jr. "Winter Texans in the Lower Rio Grande Valley." In *Economic and Business Issues of the 1980s.* Edited by J.E. Pluta. (Austin: Bureau of Business Research, 1980), p. 160.

4. See the *1992-93 Texas Almanac* for detailed information about these counties.

5. See the Department of Budget and Program Mission. *Mexican Census of Population.* (Mexico City: INEGI, 1991).

1

An Overview of Demographic and Socio-economic Conditions in the Lower Rio Grande Valley

1.1 Introduction

Before exploring the poverty/economic development relationship in the LRGV in a more rigorous fashion, it is important to have an overview of general socio-economic conditions in the region. Any strategies to eradicate poverty here must be based on a fundamental understanding of how poverty (and attendant problems) arose in the region in the first place and how changes in demographic factors have affected the region over time. From a socio-economic perspective, understanding the demographic dynamics of the region may well hold the key to structuring public policy actions so that current problems can be remedied and future ones prevented.

Understanding the infrastructure of the region is also pivotal in attempting to forecast the impact of the maquiladora phenomenon. It is important to know how industrial development in northern Mexico will affect unemployment and the level of poverty on both sides of the border. The same understanding is necessary to estimate how a proposed free trade agreement between Mexico, the United States, and Canada will affect the level of employment and the level of poverty in the region.

This chapter, then, provides a broad overview of the basic demographic changes which have occurred in the last few decades. Such information should allow us to begin to piece together the puzzle and determine why this region has been so destitute for so long.

The geographic area encompassed by this study includes the northern part of the Mexican state of Tamaulipas and the Texas counties of Cameron, Hidalgo, Starr, and Willacy, a region known as the Lower Rio

Grande Valley (LRGV -- see Figure 1.1). From earliest times, there have been distinctive similarities and differences in patterns of economic development in this region as Mexican border labor and commodities have found their way into the U.S. economy. On the Mexican side of the river, urban centers that are isolated both economically and geographically have sprung up. Because they are far from the national capital, Mexico City, and are surrounded by wasteland, these urban centers have tended to form social and economic bonds with their sister cities on the other side of the border. On the Texas side of the river, the region acts as an integrated metropolitan region with common telephone directories, an area-wide Chamber of Commerce, a roadway network, and a regional transit system.[1] These counties are the primary target of our research because they possess some of the highest poverty levels and highest unemployment levels ever recorded in the economic history of the post-World War II United States.

FIGURE 1.1 - The Lower Rio Grande Valley of Texas

TEXAS

1.2 Border Demographics

One of the most important demographic variables influencing economic conditions is population. Since 1950, the population of the state of Texas has more than doubled. However, during the last twenty years, the population of the LRGV has increased faster than the state as a whole. Table 1.1 gives population figures for both Texas and the counties that comprise the LRGV. Texas has experienced faster population growth since the end of World War II than has the nation as a whole as part of the general migration toward the Sunbelt. Census figures for 1980 and 1990 show higher population growth rates for the LRGV than for Texas with the exception of Willacy county, which does not actually front the Rio Grande River. In the last two decades, the population of Hidalgo and Starr counties more than doubled, while for Cameron county the increase has been over 85%.

The dynamics of the change in population by age groups for all of these counties are also shown in Table 1.1. By 1990, more than 35% of the resident population in the LRGV were below 18 years of age, about 10% *more* than for Texas or the United States. The group between 18 and 64 years of age made up more than 50% of the population in the LRGV, some 10% *less* than for Texas or the United States. Since 1950, the portion of the population over 65, not counting the "snowbirds" who spend from six to nine months in the area, has grown at rates up to four times that of the other age groups and currently comprises a little over 17% of the population. In Texas and the United States, the portion of the population over 65 ranges from 10% to 13%. Such differences in the relative sizes of dependent and productive populations can affect per capita incomes and the ability of a region to provide adequate social services such as schools and health care.

The increase in population in the border counties can be attributed, in part, to immigration from Mexico and from migration to the area from other parts of Texas and the United States. Overall, the counties comprising the LRGV have grown from a population of 320,484 to 701,888 since 1950, a 119% increase. Net migration accounts for over 85% of this change. Over the same period, population in the United States increased by just 65%.

Table 1.1 also reveals that the Hispanic population of the LRGV has more than doubled since 1950, with the largest gains occurring in Hidalgo and Starr counties. According to the 1990 census, 82% of the population of Cameron county, 85% of the population of Hidalgo county, 97% of the population of Starr county, and 84% of the population of Willacy county were Hispanic (most of them Mexican-American). Because of the number of illegal residents in this region, these numbers provide merely a lower

TABLE 1.1

Selected Population Characteristics, 1950-1990

	1950	1960	1970	1980	1990
US					
Total Pop.	152,271,000	180,671,000	205,052,000	227,757,000	249,633,000
% Change	15.0	18.7	13.5	11.1	9.6
Under 18 Yrs.	47,647,000	64,525,000	69,875,000	63,695,000	63,951,000
18-64 Yrs.	92,262,000	99,471,000	115,092,000	138,358,000	154,209,000
65+ Yrs.	12,362,000	16,675,000	20,085,000	25,704,000	31,473,000
Hispanic	NA	3,365,000[a]	9,230,000	14,609,000	22,354,000
Rural	61,770,000	54,054,000	53,887,000	59,495,000	64,798,000[b]
% For.Born	6.9	5.4	4.7	6.2	7.9
Births	3,632,000	4,257,850	3,731,386	3,612,258	3,909,510[b]
Deaths	1,452,454	1,711,982	1,921,031	1,989,841	2,167,992[b]
Texas					
Total Pop.	7,711,194	9,579,677	11,196,730	14,229,191	16,986,510
% Change	20.2	24.2	16.9	27.1	19.4
Under 18 Yrs.	2,596,129	2,393,666	4,639,493	4,311,445	4,835,839
18-64 Yrs.	4,601,645	5,192,185	6,518,814	8,551,744	10,434,095
65+ Yrs.	513,420	747,215	976,340	1,366,002	1,716,576
Hispanic	1,028,790[a]	1,417,810[a]	1,609,064	2,988,130	4,339,905
Rural	2,873,134	2,393,666	2,275,784	2,897,614	3,346,342
% For.Born	3.4	3.1	2.8	6.0	9.0
Births	202,965	248,574	230,624	273,433	303,418[b]
Deaths	63,083	77,231	94,335	108,018	122,874[b]
Cameron County					
Total Pop.	125,170	151,098	140,368	209,680	260,120
% Change	---------	20.7	-7.1	49.4	24.1
Under 18 Yrs.	52,913	69,919	60,639	80,400	91,840
18-64 Yrs.	66,653	73,068	67,798	109,235	140,765
65+ Yrs.	5,604	8,093	11,931	20,092	27,515
Hispanic	81,080[a]	96,744[a]	107,000	161,700	212,995
Rural	49,652	34,778	31,445	31,162	54,105
% For.Born	10.2	13.4	12.2	19.1	22.1
Births	5,189	5,426	5,322	6,927	5,873[b]
Deaths	1,189	1,042	1,088	1,378	1,576[b]

(continued)

TABLE 1.1 - continued

	1950	1960	1970	1980	1990
Hidalgo County					
Total Pop.	160,446	180,904	181,535	283,229	383,545
% Change	--------	12.8	0.3	56.0	34.4
Under 18 Yrs.	68,657	85,883	79,694	111,316	140,421
18-64 Yrs.	84,936	84,981	87,500	145,838	204,686
65+ Yrs.	6,853	10,038	14,160	26,075	38,438
Hispanic	112,422[a]	129,092[a]	143,611	230,212	326,972
Rural	68,473	52,016	46,985	59,196	90,133
% For.Born	17.1	16.1	12.6	19.9	24.7
Births	6,997	6,296	7,236	8,538	8,906[b]
Deaths	1,534	1,061	1,319	1,606	2,011[b]
Starr County					
Total Pop.	13,948	17,137	17,707	27,277	40,518
% Change	-------	22.9	3.3	54.0	48.6
Under 18 Yrs.	6,026	7,984	7,891	11,343	15,965
18-64 Yrs.	7,225	8,181	8,400	13,497	21,695
65+ Yrs.	697	972	1,416	2,437	2,858
Hispanic	12,452[a]	15,196[a]	17,330	26,428	39,390
Rural	9,956	11,302	12,031	14,952	22,569
% For.Born	6.5	7.7	9.2	21.7	34.8
Births	493	494	432	676	837[b]
Deaths	87	98	118	165	188[b]
Willacy County					
Total Pop.	20,920	20,084	15,570	17,495	17,705
% Change	-------	-4.0	-22.5	12.4	1.2
Under 18 Yrs.	9,093	9,829	6,866	6,743	6,474
18-64 Yrs.	11,070	9,226	7,380	8,984	9,255
65+ Yrs.	760	1,029	1,323	1,764	1,976
Hispanic	13,472[a]	13,734[a]	11,961	14,049	14,937
Rural	11,784	10,699	7,403	6,025	8,782
% For.Born	14.0	11.0	7.7	12.5	16.0
Births	813	626	300	259[b]	381
Deaths	168	149	112	123[b]	125

a: Hispanic surnames
b: 1988

Source: *U.S. Census, Texas Almanac, Historical Statistics of the U.S., Statistical Abstracts of the U.S., Vital Statistics of the U.S., The Texas Fact Book.*

bound. By comparison, only 25.5% of the Texas population and 8.9% of the U.S. population were Hispanic. Between 1980 and 1990 alone, the Hispanic population of the LRGV increased by more than 37% with much of the Hispanic population being foreign born. In 1980, "foreign born" represented just over 19% of the population of the LRGV. By 1990, 24% of the population was "foreign born." Such differences in ethnic composition between this area and much of the rest of Texas and the U.S. can also have important socio-economic implications.

Along with changes in the size and ethnic composition of the population, the number of families in the LRGV has also grown. Since 1970, the four counties under study have seen a 115% increase in the number of families (see Table 1.2). Over the same period, the number of families in Texas and the U.S. have grown 79% and 28%, respectively. To accommodate such an increase in family formation, housing construction in the LRGV has increased more than 130% since 1970. The figure for Texas is 83% and for the U.S., 52%. All of these statistics present a picture of a region with tremendous pressure on its infrastructure and economy. The reaction (or lack thereof) of local, state, and federal governments to this volatile situation has had significant impact on this region. In particular, government response to the problems plaguing *colonias* has sparked much debate. We say more about this below and in Chapter 3.

1.3 Socio-economic Conditions

Since the end of World War II, employment patterns in the LRGV have also changed. Agriculture, once employing as much as 50% of the labor force in the region, has declined dramatically. While this decline is consistent with an overall decline in the agricultural sector for the United States, agriculture remains an important part of the economy of the LRGV, particularly in Starr and Willacy counties where it employs more than 10% of the labor force. The percentage of workers employed in construction has also declined throughout the state, though it has risen in the United States as a whole. In Willacy county, however, construction employment has remained fairly constant. Manufacturing, a declining sector in the United States, has experienced a significant increase in the LRGV since 1950. In most of the area, the percentage of workers engaged in the manufacturing sector has at least doubled.

Services is another sector where LRGV employment patterns have differed from the nation. The service sector has grown by more than 50% in the United States since 1950. In the four counties of the LRGV the *decline* has ranged from 19% in Willacy county to 59% in Starr county, though the service sector remains one of the largest employers of labor.

TABLE 1.2

Overview of Households and Families, 1950-1990

	1950	1960	1970	1980	1990
US					
Households	43,468,000	52,799,000	63,401,000	80,776,000	93,347,000
Families	39,303,000	45,111,000	51,586,000	59,550,000	66,090,000
Housing Units	43,554,000	57,276,000	67,700,000	86,700,000	102,700,000
% Change	N.A.	31.5	18.2	28.1	18.5
Texas					
Households	2,191,000	2,778,000	3,051,000	4,929,000	6,016,000
Families	1,979,000	2,393,000	2,818,000	3,678,000	5,039,000
Housing Units	N.A.	3,153,000	3,830,000	5,549,000	7,009,000
% Change	N.A.	N.A.	21.5	44.9	26.3
Cameron County					
Households	30,496	35,663	35,432	58,785	73,278
Families	35,170	31,370	30,217	49,251	60,178
Housing Units	N.A.	42,083	41,457	65,970	88,759
% Change	N.A.	N.A.	-1.5	59.1	34.5
Hidalgo County					
Households	36,947	40,963	43,525	76,108	103,479
Families	33,240	36,431	37,771	65,139	87,912
Housing Units	N.A.	47,711	50,694	89,047	128,241
% Change	N.A.	N.A.	6.3	75.7	44.0
Starr County					
Households	2,978	3,680	4,111	6,870	10,331
Families	2,890	3,390	3,644	5,965	9,192
Housing Units	N.A.	4,489	4,988	7,833	12,209
% Change	N.A.	N.A.	11.1	57.0	55.9
Willacy County					
Households	4,901	4,573	3,808	4,790	5,049
Families	4,130	4,061	3,325	4,053	4,153
Housing Units	N.A.	5,776	4,715	5,344	6,012
% Change	N.A.	N.A.	-18.4	13.3	13.6

N.A.: not available

Source: U.S. Census.

Employment in trade has risen both throughout the country and in the LRGV. The increase in the LRGV, however, has been greater than the national average. The trade and service sector has surpassed agriculture as the primary employer in the LRGV, reflecting the importance of tourism and the Valley's role as the "gateway" to Mexico. The proposed North American Free Trade Agreement could change this distribution (see Chapter 6).

Since 1970, the labor force in Texas, Cameron county, and Hidalgo county has seen an increase in participation by females, matching the pattern in the nation as a whole. In the two predominantly rural counties, Starr and Willacy, however, females still comprise less than 40% of the work force. This could result from a lack of employment opportunities for females in these counties and contribute to the poverty that exists. For the LRGV as a whole, unemployment rates have risen since World War II and are significantly higher than rates for Texas and the United States. In Starr county, for example, nearly a quarter of the labor force was listed as unemployed in 1990, compared to a mere 5.5% for the nation as a whole.

Such high unemployment rates contribute to the fact that poverty along the Mexico-Texas border is far worse than in any other region of the United States. Bureau of the Census statistics describing both median family incomes and per capita incomes for families and individuals in the counties which comprise the LRGV indicate that a large percentage of the population is poor or very close to falling below the official poverty line. A comparison of median family incomes (see Table 1.3) illustrates the lack of improvement in the region's income levels over the last forty years. Median incomes in these border counties are lower than the median incomes for Texas as a whole and considerably lower than the rest of the United States. In 1949, the median family income for Starr county, for example, was just $1107, or a little more than one-third of the national median family income. Forty years later, median family income in Starr county had decreased to 31% of the national median family income, a loss of 5%.

Per capita income figures for Cameron, Hidalgo, Starr, and Willacy counties show the same trend. In 1960, Cameron county had the highest per capita income in the region, though it was only 55% of the national average. Starr county had the lowest per capita income measuring only 29% of the national average. This pattern changed very little during the next thirty years. By 1990, per capita income ranged from $7125 (49.4% of the national average) in Cameron county to $4,152 (28.8% of the national average) in Starr county.

Median and per capita income figures of the residents in the counties of the LRGV place many families and individuals well below or close to the federal government's definition of poverty (see Table 1.4). In 1990, for

TABLE 1.3
Per Capita and Median Family Incomes, 1949-1989

	1949	1959	1969	1979	1989
US					
Per Capita Income	$ 1,384	$ 1,849	$ 3,119	$ 7,298	$14,420
% of US median	100.0	100.0	100.0	100.0	100.0
Median Family Income	$ 3,319	$ 5,620	$ 9,586	$19,917	$35,225
% of US median	100.0	100.0	100.0	100.0	100.0
Texas					
Per Capita Income	$ 1,291	$ 1,626	$ 2,792	$ 7,205	$12,904
% of US median	93.3	87.9	89.5	98.7	89.5
Median Family Income	$ 2,273	$ 4,880	$ 8,486	$19,618	$31,553
% of US median	68.5	86.8	85.5	98.5	89.6
Cameron County					
Per Capita Income	N.A.	$ 1,242	$ 1,580	$ 4,336	$ 7,125
% of US median	N.A.	67.2	50.7	59.4	49.4
Median Family Income	$ 1,531	$ 3,216	$ 5,068	$12,931	$18,731
% of US median	46.1	57.2	52.9	64.9	53.2
Hidalgo County					
Per Capita Income	N.A.	$ 895	$ 1,523	$ 4,040	$ 6,630
% of US median	N.A.	48.4	48.8	55.3	46.0
Median Family Income	$ 1,196	$ 2,780	$ 4,776	$12,083	$17,619
% of US median	36.0	49.5	49.8	60.7	50.0
Starr County					
Per Capita Income	N.A.	$ 681	$ 1,123	$ 2,668	$ 4,152
% of US median	N.A.	36.8	36.0	36.6	28.8
Median Family Income	$ 1,107	$ 1,700	$ 3,593	$ 8,667	$10,903
% of US median	36.0	30.2	37.5	43.5	31.0
Willacy County					
Per Capita Income	N.A.	$ 985	$ 1,404	$ 4,133	$ 6,074
% of US median	N.A.	53.6	65.3	56.6	42.1
Median Family Income	$ 1,135	$ 2,902	$ 4,146	$11,443	$16,254
% of US median	33.3	51.6	43.4	57.5	46.1

N.A.: not available

Source: U.S. Census; Historical Statistics of the U.S.; Texas Almanac.

TABLE 1.4

An Overview of Poverty

	1959	1970	1980	1990
US				
Ind.in Poverty	38,682,000	25,836,552	29,608,410	31,742,864
% of Tot. Pop.	22.1	12.6	13.0	13.1
Fam.in Poverty	8,320,000	5,210,186	6,781,211	6,487,515
% of Tot. Fam.	19.6	10.1	11.4	10.0
Texas				
Ind.in Poverty	2,970,000	2,038,025	2,035,873	3,000,515
% of Tot. Pop.	31.7	18.7	14.3	18.1
Fam.in Poverty	687,965	413,804	412,076	617,981
% of Tot. Fam.	28.8	14.7	11.2	14.1
Cameron				
Ind.in Poverty	44,751	64,569	66,693	101,362
% of Tot. Pop.	35.7	46.0	31.8	39.7
Fam.in Poverty	9,890	11,634	12,805	20,544
% of Tot. Fam.	31.5	38.5	26.0	33.7
Hidalgo				
Ind.in Poverty	55,807	90,404	99,697	159,216
% of Tot. Pop.	34.8	49.8	35.2	41.9
Fam.in Poverty	13,229	15,864	18,890	32,172
% of Tot. Fam.	36.3	42.0	29.0	36.3
Starr				
Ind.in Poverty	4,869	9,721	13,797	24,150
% of Tot. Pop.	28.4	54.9	50.6	60.0
Fam.in Poverty	1,159	1,891	3,018	5,217
% of Tot. Fam.	34.2	51.9	50.6	56.5
Willacy				
Ind.in Poverty	5,832	8,906	6,188	7,848
% of Tot. Pop.	29.0	57.2	34.8	44.5
Fam.in Poverty	1,388	1,533	1,200	1,534
% of Tot. Fam.	34.2	46.1	29.6	37.6

Note: Individuals and Families are defined to be in poverty if their income falls below a government-determined minimum.

Source: Estimates from the *U.S. Census*; Texas Employment Commission.

example, nearly one-third, on average, of all families in the LRGV were below the poverty line. A similar pattern is evident for individuals. The percentage of individuals classified as being in a state of poverty was 41%, some 27% more than the nation as a whole and 24% more than the state of Texas. These percentages actually mask much of the human misery associated with poverty for they fail to adequately reflect the impact, both physically and psychologically, of such poverty on successive generations. Since 1970, the actual number of poor individuals in the LRGV has increased from 173,600 to 292,576. Yet, as a percentage of the total population in the region, the numbers show a decline from nearly 45% to 42% on average.

A closer look at the poverty rates for the LRGV reveals that problems are not equally shared between the Hispanic majority and the Anglo minority (see Table 1.5). In 1990, poor whites comprised only 10.9% of the population while 47.1% of the Hispanics in the region were classified as poor. Thus, LRGV Hispanics are more than four times as likely to be poor than are LRGV Anglos. In addition to race, sex also appears to be a segregating factor with respect to poverty. More than half of the poverty population was female in 1990, most of them Hispanic. In addition, the number of children under the age of 18 classified as poor plus the number of people over 65 classified as poor outnumbered those between the ages of 18 and 65, suggesting that women and children bear a large portion of the burden of poverty, a pattern not limited to the LRGV.

The poverty pattern of the LRGV is, in part, a function of the industrial structure of the economy of the region. As is evident from Table 1.6, the three largest sectors of the LRGV economy are agriculture, services, and trade. Much of the increase in labor force participation of the last thirty years has resulted from an increase in low wage, low skill jobs in these sectors. It is for this reason that we see both increasing labor force participation and increasing poverty. In addition, the problem may be exacerbated by labor market segregation, which would explain the larger number of females classified as below the poverty line. This will be discussed in more detail below and in Chapter 4.

As Table 1.6 demonstrates, the unemployment rates in the LRGV over the 1950-1990 period have fluctuated significantly. The average unemployment rate has moved into the double-digit range since 1980. Such high rates would not be tolerated by the electorate in most of the rest of the United States and highlights a major problem in this region. In a region where the population is constantly changing and illegal immigration is significant, voting coalitions have a much more difficult time evolving. Regions that lack stable populations have very weak collective voices politically and as the problems on the border worsen, the probability of collective action declines even further.

TABLE 1.5

Poverty Population in the Lower Rio Grande Valley by Age, Sex, and Race, 1990

	Total	Hispanic[a]	Anglo[b]	Black[c]
General Population	685,958	594,294	103,262	1,167
Pop. in Poverty	292,576	279,873	11,221	493
% of Total Poverty Pop.	42.7	47.1	10.9	42.2
Under 18 yrs.of age	133,940	130,760	2,530	202
Ages 18-64	138,737	132,663	5,376	204
Age 65 and over	19,899	16,450	3,313	87
Female Pop. in Poverty	156,162	151,437[d]	5,588[d]	410[d]
% of Total Poverty Pop.	53.40	51.76	1.91	0.14
Under 18 yrs.of age	66,120	70,721[e]	1,257[e]	168[e]
Ages 18-64	78,194	71,781[e]	2,677[e]	170[e]
Age 65 and over	11,848	8,935[e]	1,648[e]	72[e]
Male Pop. in Poverty	136,414	128,436[d]	5,633[d]	83[d]
% of Total Poverty Pop.	46.6	44.78	1.33	0.09
Under 18 yrs.of age	67,820	60,879[e]	1,267[e]	34[e]
Ages 18-64	60,543	60,879[e]	2,698[e]	34[e]
Age 65 and over	8,051	7,578[e]	1,662[e]	15[e]

a: Persons of Hispanic origin
b: Whites, not of Hispanic origin
c: Blacks, not of Hispanic origin
d: Estimated from 1987 Texas Employment Commission data.
   See R. Maril, *Poorest of Americans.*
e: Assumes age distribution across race is the same as the general population

Source: U.S. Census.

Another factor contributing to the high level of poverty in this region is the enormous differences in levels of educational attainment in the adult population relative to the level of educational attainment for all of Texas and the United States. The percentage of adults with a high school education is significantly lower in the four counties of the LRGV (see Table 1.7). Cameron county has the best record with 50% of the adult population completing high school. The worst record of 31.6% is found in Starr county. Similar figures for Texas and the U.S. as a whole are 76.2% and 72.1%, respectively. This, of course, will affect the level of occupational attainment available to families in the region.

TABLE 1.6

Employment Characteristics, 1950-1990 (as a % of labor force)

	1950	1960	1970	1980	1990
US					
Agriculture	12.0	8.1	4.1	3.1	2.6
Construction	4.6	4.9	5.8	5.8	6.2
Mining	1.4	1.0	0.6	0.9	0.6
Manufacturing	23.9	23.2	25.1	20.5	17.7
Services	21.4	22.3	25.9	29.0	32.7
Trade	18.6	19.0	19.1	20.3	21.2
% of Lab. Force Male	71.2	67.7	63.3	57.5	54.7
% of Lab. Force Fem.	28.8	32.3	36.7	42.5	45.3
Unemployment Rate	5.3	5.5	4.9	7.1	6.3
Texas					
Agriculture	16.0	11.4	4.4	2.9	1.8
Construction	8.6	10.0	7.0	8.6	6.7
Mining	3.3	3.9	2.4	3.3	2.2
Manufacturing	13.5	21.3	17.4	17.9	14.4
Services	19.7	20.3	26.6	27.3	32.6
Trade	21.4	15.4	29.9	21.8	22.4
% of Lab. Force Male	73.9	69.6	63.9	57.7	54.0
% of Lab. Force Fem.	26.1	30.4	36.1	42.3	46.0
Unemployment Rate	3.9	4.4	3.8	5.2	7.1
Cameron County					
Agriculture	26.7	19.4	9.3	4.8	2.4
Construction	8.7	5.5	7.0	7.5	5.7
Mining	0.1	0.2	0.3	0.8	0.2
Manufacturing	8.5	11.4	11.4	16.0	12.9
Services	39.6	42.0	38.5	29.0	35.8
Trade	15.3	17.1	14.0	24.3	25.5
% of Lab. Force Male	77.8	68.9	62.0	58.3	55.5
% of Lab. Force Fem.	22.2	31.1	38.0	41.7	44.5
Unemployment Rate	6.1	8.4	6.7	9.6	13.3
Hidalgo County					
Agriculture	39.0	26.8	17.0	10.9	7.6
Construction	5.4	4.7	6.1	6.5	6.6
Mining	1.5	1.7	2.0	1.2	0.9
Manufacturing	6.6	7.7	7.3	11.4	10.9

(continues)

TABLE 1.6 - continued

	1950	1960	1970	1980	1990
Hidalgo County - cont.					
Services	31.9	40.8	33.3	29.1	34.3
Trade	15.6	19.2	18.2	25.3	25.6
% of Lab. Force Male	79.1	70.1	63.6	58.2	56.9
% of Lab. Force Fem.	20.9	29.9	36.4	41.8	43.1
Unemployment Rate	8.2	6.3	6.2	12.8	14.3
Starr County					
Agriculture	43.8	39.7	23.1	21.0	14.8
Construction	7.8	4.9	6.4	6.2	9.2
Mining	8.0	3.3	3.6	4.5	1.7
Manufacturing	2.5	2.2	3.2	3.7	2.9
Services	37.0	26.5	30.2	33.8	36.4
Trade	8.0	11.0	7.9	14.9	20.6
% of Lab. Force Male	86.5	78.7	65.9	61.3	60.4
% of Lab. Force Fem.	13.5	21.3	34.1	38.7	39.5
Unemployment Rate	15.2	6.9	5.2	36.7	18.8
Willacy County					
Agriculture	50.5	42.2	32.0	20.7	14.4
Construction	4.7	3.3	3.5	6.1	4.9
Mining	1.7	1.3	1.5	2.2	1.8
Manufacturing	3.5	3.0	2.5	10.8	10.2
Services	33.9	22.6	25.7	31.5	32.9
Trade	12.9	15.2	14.1	14.3	19.6
% of Lab. Force Male	83.1	72.3	67.7	60.4	56.6
% of Lab. Force Fem.	16.9	27.7	32.3	39.6	43.4
Unemployment Rate	7.0	4.0	7.9	13.4	15.1
Ave. Unemployment Rate	9.1	6.4	6.5	18.1	15.4

Source: U.S. Census.

1.4 Mexico's Northern Border Region

The northern border region of Mexico across from the LRGV consists of ten municipalities in the state of Tamaulipas (see Table 1.8). As of 1990, their combined population totaled 1,015,167, representing 41.5% of the population of the state. This region has experienced some of the highest population growth in Mexico over the past two decades. The increase has

TABLE 1.7

Overview of Educational Achievement for Persons 25 Years and Older

	1960	1970	1980	1990
US				
Median Years Completed	10.6	12.1	12.5	12.5
% High School Graduates	26.9	52.2	66.5	76.2
% with 4 or more years of College	7.9	10.7	16.2	20.3
Texas				
Median Years Completed	10.4	11.6	12.5	N.A.
% High School Graduates	21.8	47.4	65.7	72.1
% with 4 or more years of College	8.0	10.9	16.9	20.3
Cameron				
Median Years Completed	7.9	8.5	10.3	N.A.
% High School Graduates	27.5	34.7	44.0	50.0
% with 4 or more years of College	15.1	7.4	10.5	12.0
Hidalgo				
Median Years Completed	6.3	7.3	9.3	N.A.
% High School Graduates	23.4	30.3	41.1	46.6
% with 4 or more years of College	12.2	7.3	10.8	11.5
Starr				
Median Years Completed	4.9	5.9	6.7	N.A.
% High School Graduates	19.1	21.8	26.6	31.6
% with 4 or more years of College	7.8	6.4	6.0	6.7
Willacy				
Median Years Completed	7.5	8.1	8.9	N.A.
% High School Graduates	23.2	25.6	33.6	42.9
% with 4 or more years of College	9.3	8.2	8.9	8.8

Source: *U.S. Census.*

resulted not from increasing fertility rates which have been fairly stable, but from an increase in immigration from other Mexican states (see Table 1.9). Since 1966 and the beginning of the Border Industrialization Program (see Chapter 4), net migration has declined though it still accounted for more than 50,000 people between 1980 and 1990. Chapter 5 looks more closely at the economic impact of this migration.

TABLE 1.8

Population in Mexican Border *Municipios*, 1970-1990

Municipio	1970	1980	1990
Camargo	15,416	16,014	15,043
Nuevo Laredo	151,253	203,286	219,468
Guerrero	4,249	4,191	4,510
Mier	6,193	6,382	6,244
Miguel Aleman	18,218	19,600	21,322
Gustavo Diaz O.	18,261	17,830	17,305
Reynosa	150,786	211,412	282,667
Rio Bravo	71,389	83,522	94,009
Valle Hermoso	42,287	48,343	51,306
Matamoros	186,146	238,840	303,293
TOTAL	664,198	849,420	1,015,167
% change	N.A.	27.9	19.2
Total Rural Pop.(%)	N.A.	18.4	9.6

Source: Mexican Census of Population.

Much of the population increase has been concentrated in just a few of the municipalities. By 1990, 68.5% of the population of the border municipalities couldbe found in the cities of Matamoros, Reynosa, and Camargo-Rio Bravo.[2] These three cities together have grown by approximately 270,000 people since 1970, an increase from 423,737 to 695,012 (see Table 1.10). The factors that led to this rapid population increase include a high birth rate and, perhaps more important, a large migratory flow to these cities from the interior of Mexico. Accompanying these population increases have been unemployment, underemployment, and increasing poverty. Yet, the introduction of the Border Industrial Program with its maquiladora plants was expected to ease these concerns. This issue will be explored further in Chapter 4.

TABLE 1.9

Demographic Indicators for the State of Tamaulipas

	1970	1980	1990
Population	1,456,858	1,924,484	2,249,581
% change	42.3	32.1	16.9
Total Fertility Rate[a]	2.6	2.2	2.4
Crude Birth Rate[b]	39.6	33.9	21.4
Crude Death Rate[c]	7.4	6.0	5.8
Immigration	343,859	296,922	356,392
Emigration	176,910	232,615	305,865
Net Immigration[d]	166,949	54,307	50,527

a: Average number of children a woman would have during her lifetime if she were to experience the fertility rates of the period at each age.
b: Number of births during 1 year per 1,000 persons (based on midyear population)
c: Number of deaths of children under 1 year of age per 1,000 live births in a calendar year
d: Difference between immigration and emigration

Source: Mexican Census of Population; Statistical Agenda of Mexico.

Matamoros, the largest of the Mexican border cities, is located across from Brownsville, Texas on the Gulf of Mexico. Census figures for 1990 report a 63% growth in population for the last two decades. Reynosa, the second largest Mexican border city, has also experienced rapid population growth. Its population has increased from 150,786 in 1970 to 282,667 in 1990. Reynosa is located across the Rio Grande from McAllen, Texas. Rio Bravo (and the nearby community of Camargo) is the third most important Mexican border city in the LRGV and is located across the river from Rio Grande City. The Camargo-Rio Bravo area had a combined population of 109,052 in 1990, an increase of 26.4% over the last twenty years. These three border areas, Matamoros, Reynosa, and Camargo-Rio Bravo, all have maquiladora plants which provide employment to thousands of people and serve as a magnet to attract others to the area.

TABLE 1.10

Population Characteristics of
Matamoros, Reynosa, and Camargo-Rio Bravo

	1970	1980	1990
Total Population	430,737	549,788	695,012
0-14 years	194,071	229,812	241,432
% of total	45.7	41.8	34.7
15-64 years	213,987	297,435	422,720
% of total	50.5	54.1	60.8
65 years and older	15,679	22,541	30,860
% of total	3.7	4.1	4.4
Male	211,021	272,695	343,055
0-14 years	97,883	117,105	122,622
% of total	23.1	21.3	17.6
15-64 years	105,087	144,594	205,581
% of total	24.8	26.3	29.6
65 years and older	8,051	10,996	14,852
% of total	1.9	2.0	2.3
Female	212,716	277,093	351,957
0-14 years	96,188	112,707	118,810
% of total	22.7	20.5	17.1
15-64 years	108,900	152,841	217,139
% of total	25.7	27.8	31.2
65 years and older	7,628	11,545	16,008
% of total	1.8	2.1	2.3

Source: Mexican Census of Population.

Table 1.10 divides the combined population of these three areas by sex
and age cohort for the 1970-1990 period. In 1990, 49.4% and 50.6% of the
population were male and female, respectively. The majority of the
population is of working age, 15 to 64 years old. The percentage of the
population 65 and older is growing slowly and is much lower than that
found on the U.S side of the border. The number of children below 15
years of age is declining as a percentage of the total population, a trend
that is also occurring in Texas.

The population of these Mexican border towns is characterized by low
educational attainment. (see Table 1.11) In 1990, census figures indicate
that only 28% of the population 15 years of age and over graduated from

elementary school, and only 15% of the population 18 years of age and over graduated from high school. Such figures help to explain an illiteracy rate in the northeastern part of Mexico of 7.1%, a decline of 55% since 1970. The Mexican government has recently increased its efforts to make education more readily available. However, the system lacks the efficiency found in the U.S. and often has difficulty retaining students through the six primary grades. The problem is particularly acute in rural villages where less than half of the schools even offer a complete primary education.[3] Students fortunate enough to live in a border town with a "twin city" on the U.S. side of the border (e.g. Brownsville) maintain post office boxes in the U.S. and commute to U.S. schools.[4] More affluent border families send their children to parochial boarding schools on the U.S. side of the border.

In these border cities, the provision of public services was sparse as well for the 1970-1990 period. This problem arose as people moved into the area and built small houses on land they did not own. These communities were not planned and therefore had few, if any, publicly provided utilities. In 1990, nearly 18% of the housing units lacked potable water. The same number of housing units were without electricity as well. More than 40% of the housing units also lacked sewer facilities. The number of inhabitants per household, however, has declined 25%. Lack of funds has prevented the Mexican government from adequately correcting these problems.

The economically active population in the region has increased over the last two decades from 40.4% in 1970 to 49.2% in 1990. This increase can be explained in part by the larger participation rates of women and young men. The manufacturing sector employed 25.8% of the labor force in Matamoros, Reynosa, and Rio Bravo-Camargo in 1990, much of this in the border maquilas. Given that the manufacturing sector only employed 5.3% of the labor force in 1970, it seems clear that Mexico's Border Industrialization Program, begun in 1966, has played a prominent role. Maquiladora plants rely heavily on female labor in areas that do not involve heavy industry. The agricultural sector has also declined during this period as a part of the shift toward manufacturing.

The unemployment rate for this region has fallen from 15.6% in 1970 to 3.8% in 1990.[5] The decrease can again be attributed, in part, to the increase in the number of maquiladora plants in the region as well as decreased reliance on the agricultural sector. The increase in low-wage service sector jobs coupled with the increase in urbanization could also account for some of the decline in unemployment.

The low unemployment rates given disguise a major problem in the cities -- high underemployment. Data supplied by the Census does not permit an exact count of underemployment rates, which include not only

TABLE 1.11

Social and Economic Indicators:
Matamoros, Reynosa, and Camargo-Rio Bravo

	1970	1980	1990
% Population graduated from Elem. School			
(15 years of age and over)	15.3	21.9	28.0
% Population graduated from High School			
(18 years of age and over)	10.5	13.2	15.0
% Population with College Degree			
(25 years of age and over)	4.8	7.5	8.2
% Population literate			
(15 years of age and over)	84.3	90.3	92.9
% Housing Units with:			
potable water	66.8	71.7	81.8
electricity	64.0	76.3	81.6
sewer facilities	47.1	51.6	59.6
roof made of cardboard	N.A.	N.A.	12.2
Average number of people per household	6.0	5.8	4.5
% Population Economically Active			
(over 12 years of age)	40.4	44.6	49.2
% Labor Employed in:			
agriculture	32.5	19.7	17.6
construction	4.6	6.9	8.1
manufacturing	5.3	12.9	25.8
services	10.9	14.2	23.1
trade	9.4	10.6	13.5
transportation	3.6	3.8	4.1
Unemployment Rate	15.6	6.9	3.8
% Employed working less than 32 hrs/week	N.A.	16.8	16.0
% Employed earning less than min. wage	N.A.	20.2	14.9

Source: Mexican Census of Population; Mexican Statistical Agenda.

the unemployed but also the working poor (people that either have a part-time job or are paid less than the national minimum wage). Even if this information were available, the magnitude of labor underutilization in northeastern Mexico would still be underestimated. For example, calculating the underemployment rates based on the percentage of people working less than 32 hours per week yields an underemployment rate of 16%. If we couple this estimate with the urban unemployment rate of 3.8%, the unemployment/underemployment rate for northeastern Mexico becomes 19.8% This means that during 1990 nearly 48,000 out of 241,585 workers were either unemployed or underemployed!

In summary, the LRGV can be characterized as follows:[6]

· high population growth rate
· youthful population
· strong agricultural sector
· concentration of employment in trade
· low federal employment
· manufacturing dominated by food processing and apparel
· low per capita and household income levels

The overview provided by this chapter clearly demonstrates that the high poverty rates and high unemployment in this region will not be easily remedied. The remainder of this study attempts to quantify these problems in greater detail and will assess the efficacy of alternative development strategies in eradicating or at least lessening the extent of these problems. The next chapter formalizes the measurement of poverty and describes how current public policy actions are addressing (or are not addressing) the problems in the region.

Notes

1. C. Zlatkovich. *Texas Metropolitan Area Profiles.* (Austin: Business Research Bureau, 1980): p. 41.

2. The name of the city and the name of the municipality are the same.

3. See P. Aspe and J. Beristain. *Distribution of Education and Health Opportunities and Services.* (New York: Holmes and Meier Publishers, Inc., 1984).

4. In 1981, the U.S. Supreme Court ruled that U.S. public schools must allow children of illegal aliens to attend.

5. The latter figure is based on monthly surveys conducted by the government to estimate the level of urban unemployment.

6. C. Zlatkovich, p. 45.

2

The Measurement and Analysis
of Poverty

2.1 Introduction

In February, 1993, headlines throughout the state of Texas announced that Starr County ranked among the poorest counties in the U.S. Of the nation's 3,141 counties and independent cities, Starr ranked second among the poorest. The other counties comprising the LRGV failed to do much better. Cameron, Hidalgo, and Willacy ranked 39th, 41st, and 28th -- all in the top 2% of the poorest regions in the country and among the 10 poorest counties in Texas. Nearly 42% of the entire population of the LRGV was officially classified as below the poverty line by the 1990 census (see Table 2.1).

These extraordinary poverty levels become even more incredible when one considers the efforts by the U.S. to eradicate the problem on a national level. The federal government began promoting the economic security of the population in 1935 with the passage of the Social Security Act. During the 1960s, the system expanded with the creation of a considerable number of in-kind benefit programs. As a part of this expansion, in 1964 President Lyndon Johnson's War on Poverty began. In that year there were, according to the federal government's definition, 33.2 million Americans classified as being in poverty.[1] President Johnson proposed sweeping changes through new federal programs and mandated spending to implement these programs with the intent to end poverty once and for all. The Great Society initiatives stressed services in addition to support, rehabilitation instead of relief, and training instead of dependency. Efforts were made to help the poor become self-sufficient and move off the welfare rolls. Despite these efforts, poverty continued to increase. Policy analysts called for massive welfare reform. The first

TABLE 2.1

Poverty, 1970-1990

Individuals in Poverty

	1970	1980	1990
LRGV	173,600	186,375	292,576
Texas	2,038,025	2,035,873	3,000,515
U.S.	25,836,552	29,608,410	31,742,864

Families in Poverty

	1970	1980	1990
LRGV	30,922	35,913	59,467
Texas	413,804	412,076	617,981
U.S.	5,210,186	6,781,211	6,487,515

Median Family Income

	1970	1980	1990
LRGV	$ 4,396	$11,281	$17,853
Texas	8,486	19,618	30,129
U.S.	9,586	19,917	32,191

Source: U.S. Census.

major effort to reform the welfare system came in 1969 with President Nixon's Family Assistance Program (FAP) which called for a guaranteed minimum income. The FAP was not adopted but it did lead to legislation for the Earned Income Tax Credit (EITC). This 1975 law gave "tax refunds" to low-income families with at least one member who had worked during the past year. Again, no additional gains were made in reducing the poverty rate and other reform efforts by both the Carter and Reagan adminstrations failed to be adopted.

TABLE 2.2

Welfare and Poverty in Texas, 1960-1990
(Expenditures are in 1960$; rates are %)

	1960	1970	1980	1990
Poverty Rate	31.7	18.8	14.7	18.1
% change	----	-40.7	-21.8	23.1
Welfare Expenditures	$212,768,119	$422,456,119	$669,788,630	$962,635,909
% change	----	98.6	58.5	43.7

Source: *U.S. Census*; *Texas Almanac.*

After more than twenty years of continuing to introduce new programs and after spending hundreds of billions of dollars on these programs, 33.5 million Americans were still, again by the federal government's definition, poor in 1990. More than 3 million of these poor lived in Texas where welfare spending continues to rise. Table 2.2 shows that welfare expenditures in Texas in 1970 and 1980 increased nearly twice as fast as poverty rates decreased. In 1990, the poverty rate in Texas actually increased by 23%! In Texas, at least, welfare spending has clearly been ineffective in combating the problem.

The South's share of these millions of poor Americans can typically be found in rural areas. This is true in Texas as well. Most of the 61 counties in Texas with poverty rates twice that of the national average lie some distance from major metropolitan areas. According to the 1990 census, sixteen of these poorest counties cluster along Texas' border with Mexico.

Clearly, many of these poor reside in south Texas. Johnson's War on Poverty had a significant impact on the LRGV in the 1960s, though not perhaps always the intended one. The expansion of existing programs for the poor and the creation of new ones were intended to ease the burden on those in need and it was also hoped that these programs would provide thousands of jobs to LRGV workers. Special emphasis was given to job creation in the governmental sector. Before embarking on a discussion of how poverty elimination programs have worked in the LRGV, it is necessary to carefully define poverty and construct an appropriate poverty index.

2.2 Defining Poverty

Any definition of poverty will obviously have important ramifications in not only counting the number of poor, but in determining appropriate policy actions to alleviate the problem as well. Identifying the poor is not a simple task, though numerous attempts by scholars and government bureaucrats have been made. Michael Harrington, in his classic study of poverty in America, offered the following definitions of poverty:

> Poverty should be defined in terms of those who are denied the minimum levels of health, housing, food, and education that our present stage of scientific knowledge specifies as necessary for life as it is now lived in the United States. Poverty should be defined psychologically in terms of those whose place in the society is such that they are internal exiles who, almost inevitably, develop attitudes of defeat and pessimism and who are therefore excluded from taking advantages of new opportunities. Poverty should be defined absolutely, in terms of what man and society should be.[2]

The Social and Economic Committee of the European Common Market defined the poor as "those individuals and families...whose resources are so small that they find themselves excluded from the mode of life, the normal patterns and activities, of the countries in which they live."[3]

A more formal definition was proposed in 1965. The United States Department of Agriculture conducted a survey of the expenditures of families of three or more people. This landmark study reported that the average family spent about one-third of its income on food. Using this study and retaining the assumption that families spend one-third of their income on food, Mollie Orshansky created the government's official definition of poverty. The cost of a basic and nutritionally sound food plan was then used to determine the minimum amount of income necessary to avoid being classified as poor, i.e., three times the cost of the food plan. This measure was then indexed by the Consumer Price Index to determine changes in the poverty line from year to year and implicitly assumes that the consumption behavior that was valid for most families in 1965 should be valid for families over time, thereby yielding an absolute index of poverty. Considerable debate exists as to whether poverty should be measured this way. Arthur Burns, serving as one of Richard Nixon's top domestic advisors, even argued that poverty was only an "intellectual concept" defined by "artificial statistics."[4]

Despite such skepticism, two general paradigms exist which define poverty. They are: as an absolute metric (like the measure discussed above), and as a relative metric. The "absolutists" define poverty as an absolute condition. This metric follows the Orshansky notion that poverty is the inability to command a market basket of goods such as food, clothes, and shelter that comprise the most basic necessities of life.   Because necessities are a normative concept varying greatly between societies and across cultures, many economists have argued that poverty should be measured as a relative concept.   These "relativists" define poverty as a function of one's income relative to some measure of society's general well-being. One "relative" definition considers poverty as "any household earning less than one-half of the median personal income".[5] Another relative measure is found by dividing the observed income distribution into quartiles and examining the income held by the lowest quartile.[6] The definition adopted by the United States government embraces elements of both measures. Orshansky refers to it as "relatively absolute". Relative because it is based on the average portion of income spent on food for all families and absolute because the poverty levels are based on expenditures for food required to meet minimum nutritional standards.[7]

The policy implications arising from the relative vs. absolute debate in defining poverty are far reaching. If poverty is defined as an absolute level, then an economic policy which has "trickle down" consequences may well be appropriate. That is, as a society increases its standard of living across the board, those at the bottom of society are lifted out of poverty. By contrast, defining poverty as a relative index implies that a country (or state or county or city) can never entirely lift its citizens out of poverty by pursuing particular policies, for example, by pursuing economic growth. As has been pointed out, ultimately it is hard to say whether poverty is or should be an absolute or relative concept.[8]

Researchers have discussed the merits of both types of definitions, and several recent studies, based on public opinion surveys, suggest that most Americans think about poverty in terms of a hybrid concept embracing many of the characteristics mentioned above.[9] This is an important point, since recent econometric research seems to suggest that policies to alleviate poverty may be implemented in part as a response to the public's perception of poverty.[10] The economic proposals put forward by President Clinton in February, 1993, were based, in part, on the public's renewed awareness of increasing poverty and the broad concerns that something needed to be done.

At this point, it might be helpful to review the United States government's method for setting the official poverty line which determines who is actually eligible for government benefits. The most straight forward method, as explained in the *New Palgrave Dictionary of Economics*, is to determine a basket of goods x, at a price level p, and set poverty equal to:

$$(1 + h) \, p \, x$$

Here, the parameter *h* represents a "fudge" factor, which defines inefficient expenditure or waste.[11] In other words, it accounts for commodities not inclusive in the basket of goods *x*. In applying this methodology, the bundle of commodities that comprise the Consumer Price Index (CPI) can be used as the basket of goods necessary for maintaining subsistence levels. Poverty could be defined, therefore, as the level of subsistence at which people cannot afford the specified basket of goods *x*. Thus, the CPI bundle of goods would serve as an indication of a minimum subsistence level, and therefore, a level at which poverty starts. The problem is, however, that as the CPI changes over time (from year to year), the definition of poverty will change also. This suggests that the CPI bundle of goods is not a precise instrument for determining poverty lines.

The Bureau of Labor Statistics is responsible for constructing the CPI. Naturally they began defining the poverty line as well. The poverty line was adjusted annually based on changes in the cost of its food basket up until 1969. Since that time, the poverty line has been increased according to changes in the entire Consumer Price Index, not just the food component. There is a serious problem with using the CPI as a poverty line indicator, however.

The CPI was once calculated in a way that gave considerable weight to the housing component. This greatly overstated increases in housing costs which were reflected in large changes in the overall CPI. The attendant poverty line was also overstated as a result. The CPI was revised in 1983 and again in 1987 to correct the housing cost problem and medical care cost problems, but subsequent adjustments to the poverty line have been based on the overstated values generated between 1969 and 1983. One result is that the official poverty line is higher than it would be if it had been adjusted consistently using current CPI calculations. The newest guidelines for 1993 place the poverty level for a family of four at $12,675 per year.

Public policy will only be effective in combating poverty if we have a clear characterization of just who the poor actually are. This problem is particularly acute in the *colonias* that have sprouted up on both sides of the Mexico-Texas border. In particular, the poor in the LRGV defy official definitions.

2.3 The Poor in Northeastern Mexico

Unfortunately, in this region there is a paucity of statistical data that show how many of the children, the elderly, the employed, or the underemployed are considered poor. There are also few data available that report what percentage of Mexican families find themselves below the poverty line. However, it is estimated that approximately 51% of the people living in the region are poor, particularly those who live in rural areas. A great percentage of the poor urban dwellers live in what are referred to as lost cities (*ciudades perdidas*) of misery that surround the urban areas of the cities. It is also estimated that among the poor, 53.8% of the family heads work in agriculture, 19.7% are in the industrial sector, 15.4% are in the service sector, and 20% are either unemployed or underemployed. In addition, 12.2% had not finished elementary school and 53.7% had no formal education or job skills.[12] A substantial portion of the population of the region have immigrated to the region from other Mexican states.[13]

As the population continues to grow, more education and health care have to be provided and more employment opportunities must be created. The government does provide schooling for children and membership in public health institutions for individuals in northeastern Mexico. However, there are still thousands of individuals who will never reach the sixth grade, thousands of children who are unable to find a place in elementary schools, and an illiteracy rate of 7.1% (see Table 1.11). In the case of public health, even when modern facilities are expanded, there are thousands of persons who do not receive modern medical care and still rely on folk cures and herbs. Even the most superficial trip through the cities of the region reveals large numbers of individuals living in cardboard dwellings and other substandard structures.

Unemployment persists as does concern about the larger problem of high underemployment. As mentioned in Chapter 1, accurate information about the extent of underemployment is very difficult to obtain, but a combined unemployment/underemployment rate of nearly 20% would not be surprising! Turnover in the maquiladora plants is extremely high as is the employment of women. Both contribute to the unstable employment patterns evident in the region.

The large pool of unemployed and underemployed people exerts downward pressure on wages and also affects the income distribution, already highly skewed in this region. Moreover, in addition to the existence of "relative" poverty, many families have income earners receiving less than the minimum wage. To the extent that the minimum wage is supposed to represent a "well-being" threshold, this suggests that a considerable portion of the population has not achieved this level of well-being. Moreover, the minimum wage is not adequate to cover the "basic needs" of a standard family since it decreased in real terms during the 1980s. These factors, coupled with the high concentration of income among the rich in the area, suggests that the region is also plagued by large differences in the distribution of food consumption, causing serious problems with malnutrition.

Social program expenditures in northeastern Mexico have favored a particular segment of the population in these cities. Thus, a vast majority of the total population has been kept marginally out of poverty (sociologists have referred to them as *marginados* -- slum inhabitants, peasants and unorganized workers). In addition, of the 1986 total public sector budget of the state of Tamaulipas, only 7.4% was spent on social development and 3.4% on environmental and regional development.

The National Solidarity Program is one of the newest instruments that the Mexican federal government has implemented to combat the worst aspects of the unequal income distribution. The program's intent is to raise the quality of life of individuals in rural communities. It appears to have already benefitted poor communities across the entire country (including its northeastern part) through the introduction of electricity, paved streets, and sewer systems.

The prospects of greater trade, foreign investment and high rates of economic growth should allow these social policies to become more intensified and to permit the channelling of resources to the population in rural areas.[14] The current Mexican government has demonstrated a continued growing concern for the poor through social programs such as public health, education, and housing. Nevertheless, the effort must be continued to supply more ammunition in the war against poverty. Since the border between northern Mexico and Texas has been described as both a "barrier and a membrane", any poverty that exists in northeastern Mexico will affect poverty levels on the Texas side of the border.[15]

2.4 The Poor in South Texas

Poverty permeates the LRGV. It has been pervasive and endemic. The poor constitute more than 59,000 families, almost half the population. These figures, of course, include only people officially counted as part of the population. Many *colonia* residents are illegal aliens and avoid census takers when possible. Nominal family income in south Texas has increased threefold since the War on Poverty began, but it remains only 55% of U.S. median family income (see Table 2.1). The Center on Budget and Policy Priorities, a bipartisan research group, has argued that rural housing for the poor lags far behind that found in the cities.[16] This is particularly true in the LRGV. Table 2.3 lists basic features of the households of the LRGV and Texas. As is apparent, many houses lack heat, complete plumbing, and the usual kitchen facilities. More than 14% of the households lack telephones. In fact, many entire *colonias* have no telephones. Nearly 13% have no transportation and must rely on either friends, relatives, or inadequate public transportation.

TABLE 2.3

Housing Characteristics, 1990 (%)

	Cameron	Hidalgo	Starr	Willacy	LRGV	Texas
No Heat	0.7	0.7	2.4	0.3	0.7	0.2
No Vehicle	13.5	11.7	16.9	13.4	12.7	8.1
No Telephone	14.0	13.3	31.3	14.4	14.5	7.5
Lack Complete Plumbing	3.8	6.2	9.9	6.6	5.5	1.2
Lack Complete Kitchens	2.1	3.6	7.4	2.6	3.2	1.2

Source: U.S. Census.

Some groups of individuals are more likely to fall into the poverty category than others. We can think of poverty as a hazardous activity and the hazard is more dangerous for some cohorts in the population than for others. Table 1.5 shows, for instance, that Hispanics in the LRGV were approximately four times more likely to be poor than were LRGV Anglo-Whites in 1990. This was due, in part, to their inability to speak English well. Table 2.4 shows that almost three-fourths of the population of the LRGV spoke a language other than English at home in 1990. Of this group, more than half did not speak English well. Language barriers, particularly among the young, pose a real threat to educational and economic advancement. Many of the children require remedial help in school to help overcome these difficulties.

The poor may be divided into four additional major groups: the elderly, children, employed working-age adults, and unemployed working-age adults. Each of these groups possesses problems that need to be addressed by different programs as is discussed below. First, the elderly, those 65 years of age and older, made up 10.1% of the population of the LRGV in 1990. Of the elderly, about 28% were classified as poor (see Table 2.5). This represents a 40% increase since 1970. Relatively few elderly people hold jobs, and that obviously is the main cause of poverty among the elderly if no pension provision or retirement planning was done during their working years. Some of the elderly poor are willing and able to hold regular jobs, but most cannot. An increasing number of elderly people are electing to live alone and must support themselves. The best and often

TABLE 2.4A

Persons Who Speak a Language Other Than English at Home, 1990

	Total	Ages 5-17	Age 18 & Over
Texas	3,970,304	974,282	2,996,022
% of State pop.	23.4		
Cameron	185,016	57,281	127,735
% of Cnty.pop.	71.1		
Hidalgo	283,861	90,919	192,942
% of Cnty.pop.	74.0		
Starr	34,854	11,563	22,692
% of Cnty.pop.	84.5		
Willacy	12,854	4,046	8,808
% of Cnty.pop.	72.6		

Source: U.S. Census.

TABLE 2.4B

Persons Who Do Not Speak English Well, 1990

	Total	Ages 5-17	Age 18 & Over
Texas	1,766,835	391,661	1,766,835
% of State pop.	10.4		
Cameron	94,719	26,636	68,083
% of Cnty.pop.	36.4		
Hidalgo	151,101	45,369	105,732
% of Cnty.pop.	39.4		
Starr	22,347	7,053	15,294
% of Cnty.pop.	55.2		
Willacy	6,877	1,962	4,915
% of Cnty.pop.	38.8		

Source: U.S. Census.

TABLE 2.5

Poverty in the Lower Rio Grande Valley, 1970-1990

	1970	1980	1990
Cameron			
Total	64,009	66,046	101,362
under age 18	32,790	32,935	45,525
65 and older	5,249	5,046	7,141
Hidalgo			
Total	89,838	99,081	159,216
under age 18	45,879	49,627	72,907
65 and older	6,026	7,240	10,559
Starr			
Total	9,713	13,698	40,264
under age 18	4,612	6,623	10,743
65 and older	815	1,166	1,521
Willacy			
Total	8,865	6,065	17,631
under age 18	4,502	2,863	3,618
65 and older	2,057	623	687
LRGV			
Total	172,425	184,890	318,473
under age 18	87,783	92,048	132,793
65 and older	14,147	14,075	19,908

Source: U.S. Census.

the only practical way to help the aged poor is to give them some form of income support. Their health-care needs normally are more expensive and also must be met. This particular problem is not confined to the LRGV.

Perhaps the most tragic victims of poverty are the children. More than half of the LRGV population classified as poor in 1970 were children under 18 years of age. By 1990, the absolute number had grown, though they represented only about 42% of the poor (see Table 2.5). This fact is of special social concern, because children who grow up in poverty are denied opportunities from the start and are unfairly hindered in preparing themselves for productive adult lives. Furthermore, they are much more likely to stay in poverty throughout their lives. Yet these children are U.S. citizens, though they may have parents who are not. Given this, it becomes increasingly imperative that they receive the help that will prevent a "culture of poverty" from becoming intergenerational. These children have special needs beyond those which can be provided for by giving their families higher incomes. In particular, health care, compensatory education, and vocational training are essential to provide permanent freedom from poverty for this cohort. The Clinton administration has pledged to increase spending in such important areas as the Head Start program, but this must be accompanied by a program to impress upon the parents of these children the need to enroll their children in such programs. Some of the programs in the Valley have openings that are not filled because parents either fail to enroll their children or are unaware of the benefits Head Start provides. Other communities have waiting lists because funds have been cut.

The working poor constitute another major group in poverty. Most of those employed in maquiladoras in northern Mexico and many illegals working as laborers in south Texas fall into this category. Being employed does not necessarily guarantee an income adequate enough to stay above the poverty line. Many poor people under 65 years of age are employed at least part time. For these people and their families poverty results from low-paying jobs as well as from large families and from long spells of unemployment. The working poor also experience other labor market difficulties. Many leave the work force voluntarily because of illness or disability or because they become discouraged about the prospects of finding a job and simply stop looking. In 1990 approximately one-half of poor family heads of households worked.[17] Many poor families had two or more wage earners in at least some period of the year and yet still remained poor.

The problems for the working poor are frequent joblessness, low wages and inadequate skills. In the LRGV the agriculture, service, and trade sectors employ the majority of workers (see Table 1.6). Employment in these sectors can be sporadic and sensitive to the overall economies of both the U.S. and Mexico. In the last decade, agriculture in particular has suffered from the vagaries of the weather. Prior to 1983, the Texas citrus industry grossed $100 million. Catastrophic freezes eliminated many of the orange and grapefruit trees along with the jobs that the industry supplied. The fields have been replanted but are a few years away from their former productivity. Gross receipts for producers totalled only $12.6 million in 1992.[18]

Wages are also low. Workers in rural areas have generally earned less than their urban counterparts. Average nominal weekly wages in the LRGV in 1980 were $176.20, 65.6% of those of the state. By 1990, this figure had increased to $265.35, less than 80% of the state's nominal average weekly wage and barely half of the average weekly wage earned in the more urban Dallas county. A worker supporting a family of four at this weekly wage would have to be employed forty-eight weeks of the year to make the $12,675 necessary to remain above the poverty level. Yet the average unemployment rate of the Valley is more than 15%. Those workers making less than the average weekly wage are at risk. If this same worker earned only the minimum wage of $4.25 an hour, his yearly income would be $8,840 -- less than 70% of the poverty level income.

The low wages that persist in the LRGV reflect, in part, the lack of education and training of many Valley residents. Less than half the people in these four counties have completed high school and far fewer still have attended college. Nationally, Hispanic youth, who comprise most of the young population of the Valley, have a more than 40% dropout rate.[19] Educational spending per pupil is 92% of the state average but this has not provided the results needed to prepare the young to be economically productive.[20] They are not acquiring the skills necessary for today's labor market which requires more education than in past generations. Without this education, the young will be forced into an "economic underworld" rooted in poverty. Poorly educated young people simply have greater difficulty in more complex, modern environments. This suggests that the plight of the working poor could be alleviated to some extent by finding new ways to encourage the young to complete their education, by implementing training programs which allow the young to acquire marketable skills, and by better employment programs that streamline the operation of the labor market, increase the productivity of low-income workers, and create opportunities for employment and advancement.

2.5 Employment Patterns

The unemployed and underemployed are the last major group of poverty victims we discuss. It is well known that the vast majority of the labor force in most developing countries (and in all countries prior to the 19th century) work or worked in the agricultural sector. In an agricultural economy, much of the work is labor intensive. Most of the developing country's labor is devoted to the basic task of feeding the population. Developed countries are able to divert far more of their productive resources into other pursuits. In the U.S. and Canada, only 4% and 7%, respectively, of all employed persons work in the agriculture sector or in fishing and mining. This is compared to more than 70% in India. The LRGV has retained many of the characteristics of a developing country. The average number of people employed in the agricultural sector has remained nearly four times higher than the national average. As mentioned above, this reliance on agriculture has caused increased under-

and unemployment. These problems will be exacerbated with the full implementation of the North American Free Trade Agreement (see Chapter 6).

The manufacturing sector has been the traditional backbone of a developed industrial economy. In 1990, about one-fourth of all the jobs in the United States were in manufacturing and construction. However, these sectors employed less than 16% of the labor force in the Valley. With the advent of new technologies, employment in manufacturing has demanded greater technical skills. This has reduced unskilled labor's share of total employment and increased the importance of improved education and training mentioned above.

Probably the most striking change in employment in the developed countries such as the United States in recent years has been the rapid expansion of the service sector. This has been true in the LRGV as well where more than a third of the labor force was employed in the service sector in 1990. These jobs, however, have traditionally been low wage, low productivity ones. The changes in the type of jobs have also been accompanied by changes in composition of the labor force. During the twentieth century, the percentage of women, especially of married women in the total labor force has increased. In 1990, roughly 45% of the U.S. labor force was made up of women. This was true of the Valley as well. In many cases, the employment of women has helped to increase employment in the service sector. It has also provided necessary supplemental income to the increasing number of families facing poverty.

Fiscal and monetary policy also affect unemployment by stimulating or depressing business activity. These policies, however, guide the economy as a whole, and they are too broad to be aimed at specific industries or population groups that need special help. Programs to create new jobs, to upgrade workers' skills, or to retrain workers for new types of jobs are often adopted to fill these needs. In the United States, the Comprehensive Employment and Training Act (CETA) of 1973 provided federal grants to state and local governments to meet the training needs of unemployed and underemployed persons. It was replaced by a smaller job-training program in 1982, the Job Training Partnership Act (JTPA). These programs have had limited success in the LRGV, in part because many of the very poor lack U.S. citizenship. President Clinton has pledged to institute new programs to aid in worker training, particularly in areas such as south Texas.

Another focus of government has been wages. Congress set a minimum wage allowable by law as part of the Fair Labor Standards Act (FLSA) of 1938. An increase in the minimum wage was passed by the Congress, despite the threat of veto by President Bush. The amendment to FLSA increased the minimum wage from $3.35 per hour to $3.85 per hour on

April 1, 1990 and to $4.25 per hour on April 1, 1991. The Clinton administration has suggested increasing the minimum wage by 10% and indexing it to inflation. The idea is to ensure that employed workers receive at least a subsistence income, though it is sometimes claimed that this practice favors currently employed union workers and increases unemployment among the young by raising the cost of hiring unskilled workers. If this is true, the lack of skills of much of the LRGV labor force would be hurt by any attempt to set wages at a level higher than productivity would warrant. In addition, many of the jobs available in the Valley are either part time or part of an informal service sector and are simply not affected by laws setting minimum wages.

Finally, many governments seek to ameliorate the often devastating effects of long-term unemployment through unemployment insurance and social welfare programs. Concepts that link laziness and poverty are generally unfounded. A landmark study published in 1981 concluded that labor supply does not decrease with increases in income transfer programs.[21] Many of those unemployed of working age cannot find jobs because of such factors as personal handicaps or a scarcity of jobs. Available data suggest that illness and family responsibilities are the main reasons why poor people do not work. Children not only increase income requirements and the likelihood of poverty, but also keep mothers from working and thereby limit available income. Some of the unemployed poor could and should be encouraged to seek employment. For most, however, some kind of assistance is necessary. This is once again particularly true for the LRGV.

2.6 Alleviating Poverty: Public Policy in the U.S.

Since World War II and the Roosevelt era, the term welfare state has been used to refer to the government's responsibility for the economic and social well-being of the public. Public assistance programs originally were instituted with the aim of lessening the hardships caused by unemployment, disability, and old age and the securing for all, regardless of income, adequate medical care and other essential services. The issue of poverty and how to relieve it is complex. Governments have long attempted to expand economic and social opportunities and health care for citizens, but the programs tended to be limited and selective of the issues. An historical perspective on these programs is given in Table 2.6.

To solve the poverty puzzle, the policymaker must keep in mind the wisdom expressed in the thought "to give a man a fish, makes him a beggar; to teach him to fish, makes him a fisherman." It is well known that in the short run, cash support can relieve immediate personal crises.

TABLE 2.6

Historical Summary of Significant Public Assistance Programs

Year	Program
Roman Empire	Military Pensions
1777	U.S. Military Pensions
1880	German Old Age & Sickness Insurance
1911	Great Britain National Insurance
1920	U.S. Pension Plan for Federal Employees
1930	Swedish Health & Unemployment Insur.
1935	U.S. Social Security Legislation
1937	U.S. Railroad Retirement Act
1951	U.S. Aid to the Disabled
1964	U.S. Economic Opportunity Act
1965	U.S. Medicaid & Medicare Amendment
1973	U.S. Comprehensive Employment & Training Act (CETA)
1974	U.S. Employee Retirement Income Security U.S. Supplemental Security Income U.S. Project Developmental Continuity U.S. Basic Education Skills Program
1981	U.S. Aid to Families with Dependent Children
1982	U.S. Job Training Program

Such views are dangerously myopic, however, when battling persistent poverty. Public policy programs must enable individuals and families to get off social and welfare programs and become self-sustaining.

As mentioned above, public assistance programs have proliferated since the New Deal in the 1930s. The United States has developed an intricate series of programs to help the economically disadvantaged. The system developed by the U.S. government is by no means comprehensive and is based on the assumption that special-purpose programs are necessary to cover the diverse needs of the poor. Special interest groups have also had a significant impact on the evolution of these public programs. Consequently, some programs address only one particular problem in dealing with the poor, others overlap in their coverage.

Four general types of programs exist in the United States: cash support, direct provision of necessities (food, shelter and medical care), programs aimed at preventive and compensatory help for children and young people, and programs which attempt to restructure existing institutions and to help the poor deal with the institutions. The first of these, income-support programs, are the main form of assistance to the poor. Because poverty is usually defined as the lack of adequate income, cash subsidies attack it most directly. One problem with cash support is that payments to employable persons may diminish their incentive to work. Another problem is that income subsidies may not be used to provide basic sustenance as intended, but may be spent on other things. Finally, public opinion plays a significant role. The public may vote to pay allowances to poor people who are in training programs, but may not wish to support the idle poor. Cash-income support programs include unemployment insurance; workers compensation; old age, survivors', and disability insurance; public assistance; and pensions. Due to public sentiment against income payments to employable persons and those who are not legal residents of the U.S., these programs aim primarily at legal residents who are outside the work force. More comprehensive programs have also been proposed to distribute income subsidies based on need rather than on labor-force status. These programs include guaranteed income, a negative income tax, and family allowances. To date, Congress has failed to implement any of these programs.

Another program is the direct provision of necessities. These types of programs provide goods and services directly to the needy to supplement their cash income. In-kind aid is normally more politically palatable than cash; also some proponents argue that the government is a better judge of the needs and priorities than the individual. The necessary goods often are a result of surpluses of the aid to farmers' programs and may not be available on the market.

Low-cost housing, for example, is not profitable to construct. The government may be able to provide housing services more inexpensively than the private sector. This is particularly true in the areas where the magnitude of poverty limits the ability of municipalities and county governments to provide basic services. Because of such problems in the LRGV of South Texas, the poor have limited housing choices. *Colonia* residents buy lots which they can barely afford on their limited incomes and then build their own houses. The developer rarely furnishes infrastructure; police and fire protection are sporadic; and garbage service is nonexistent.

The government offers other services not so much to alleviate the suffering of today's poor as to give their children a chance to escape from poverty. Helping families to avoid having more children than they desire is one of the most productive ways of eliminating poverty. Proper care for mother and child is also extremely important, so that the young will be healthy. The federal government also provides some compensatory education from preschool to college for children of the poor.

One federally financed education program is Project Head Start, mentioned earlier. It serves the developmental needs of handicapped children and children from low-income families. A broad range of services is provided to these children and their families in an attempt to improve their intellectual development, self-esteem, and physical and mental health. The Administration for Children, Youth and Families of the U.S. Department of Health and Human Services supports this program. Local agencies administer the program which provides educational services to the parents who participate in the children's activities and serve on advisory boards. Head Start also provides medical and dental care. In addition, healthful meals are served to the children, and education on nutrition is provided to the family. Social service needs are assessed, and families are guided to the necessary helping agencies. The program began in 1965 with 3,300 centers serving more than 550,000 children. Since then the number of centers and the numbers of enrollees has declined. In 1982 about 396,000 children, or 20% of the 2 million eligible, were enrolled in Head Start programs, 375,000 of them in year-round programs. Out of this Head Start program several other federally funded programs have emerged, e.g., Project Developmental Continuity, which was begun in 1974 to assure a continuity of services to Head Start children during their transition to elementary schools. The Basic Educational Skills program was begun in 1979 to extend the continuity of services through the elementary grades. Programs intended to restructure institutions or to improve the ability of the poor to work with existing institutions are meant to attack the causes of poverty rather than merely its symptoms. Such programs are generally aimed at offering more opportunities to the employable poor. The emphasis is on economic institutions, although the fact has been increasingly recognized that controlling noneconomic institutions, such as political parties and schools, is often a prerequisite to economic opportunity.

These programs fall into three groups. First, some programs seek to give the individual a competitive edge in the labor market through training, placement, and rehabilitation and through incentives to private employers to hire the disadvantaged. Second, some programs attempt to restructure the labor market by establishing a minimum wage, offering public employment, and combating discrimination. Third, other programs are designed to redevelop depressed urban and rural areas suffering from chronic unemployment.

The various strategies for helping the poor complement each other. Not only must today's poverty be alleviated through cash and in-kind aid, but it must be prevented in the future by providing poor young people with better preparation and, therefore, a better chance at success in the job market. Isolating the impact of these programs upon beneficiaries is not always easy. Birth control and maternal care, designed to give children a better start in life, also leave the mother in a better position to contribute to her own support. Similarly, the difference between cash subsidies and rehabilitative programs is often blurred: for instance, stipends are necessary for the poor if they are to complete an effective training program.

As discussed above, public assistance programs, are commonly called "social, public, or welfare services." They provide cash or other benefits for particular categories of the financially needy. In the United States, welfare programs showed significant growth after the end of World War II when a rapid increase in welfare costs occurred during the 1960s and 1970s. The federal government funds and administers one of the four major public assistance programs -- Supplementary Security Income (SSI); though a few states provide additional SSI payments. The other three -- Aid to Families with Dependent Children (AFDC), General Assistance, and Emergency Assistance -- are funded by a combination of federal, state, and local monies. However, these programs are administered by the states and localities, which set up their own schedules of eligibility and benefits. A major drawback is that these schedules vary widely with great disparities existing in assistance levels from state to state. All program applicants are given a means test, from which eligibility is determined according to income and assets. The definition of assets, however, differs among the states and the federal welfare agencies. In addition, recipients must usually be U.S. citizens.

The War on Poverty was formally declared in 1964 in the form of the Economic Opportunity Act (EOA). It was an attempt to break the cycle of poverty affecting nearly 35 million Americans.   The act rejected the alternative concept of direct subsidies and was signed into law in August 1964. In attempting to prepare the poor for successful competition in an expanding economy, it combined new and existing programs of services by professionals - VISTA, Neighborhood Youth Corps, Job Corps, College Work Study, and Head Start - with the Community Action Programs (CAP) designed to involve recipients with "maximum feasible participation." However, almost immediately the program encountered competition from local political welfare establishments for control over CAP. All of this, combined with inadequate funding and competition for funds from the Vietnam War effort, created many problems for the program.

The largest and most expensive of all the welfare programs, AFDC, is intended to cover the minimum costs of providing care for dependent children (more than $8.5 billion in 1981). This program is available for children in need who have lost the support of a parent because of death, prolonged absence, or incapacity and to the parents or guardians with whom the children live. The program was first enacted in Illinois in 1911, with the legislation providing funds to enable widows and deserted women to care for their children. Aid to Families with Dependent Children was included in the Social Security Act of 1935 as a joint federal-state assistance program. Under the program the federal government provides matching grants to the states with each state administering its own program. No federal minimum benefit level has been established; thus, benefits vary widely from state to state.

These federal-state programs were funded by grants from the federal government. Additional programs were enacted for old-age assistance and as aid to the blind as part of the Social Security Act of 1935. In 1951, Aid to the Permanently and Totally Disabled was enacted. Supplemental Security Income (SSI) replaced state-administered programs and provided minimum cash income to aged, blind, and disabled people.

Another program is based upon general assistance. The General Assistance Program is for people who are ineligible for programs in other federal categories. Eligibility is based on a state-defined need and is verified by a means test that considers all of an individual's income and assets. In some states, the possibility of aid from relatives is included. Benefits range from cash payments to groceries and shelter and are administered by state or local authorities. Emergency Assistance in some states is available for specified emergencies to adults eligible for SSI and to destitute families with minor children.   To qualify, adults must experience sudden emergencies that essentially deprive them of the means to stay alive and healthy. In the case of families, emergency aid is limited to 30 days in a 12-month period. Help is in the form of cash, in kind, or in voucher form. The emergency assistance program operates in 25 states.

In addition to the four major programs, the public assistance system also includes housing allowances, Medicaid, and food stamps. Other programs include school lunches, the Work-Incentive Program (which provides job placement, training, or public service employment), an earned income-tax credit for low-income workers with a child in the household and the Home Energy Assistance Program, which supplies supplementary fuel or utility payment during the heating season to certain public assistance and SSI recipients. Social services also include daycare centers, foster and protective care, family planning, and services to the mentally retarded and drug and alcohol abusers. In addition, there are hundreds of private, charitable institutions which also provide many types of assistance for the impoverished. Many of these have played some role in dealing with poverty in the LRGV.

2.7 Alleviating Poverty: Public Policy in the LRGV

Many of the programs mentioned above are administered through the Texas Department of Human Services (TDHS). The LRGV comprises a part of the 26-county Region 8. This particular region is the third largest in Texas and consistently has among the highest monthly ADFC and food stamp caseloads. Table 2.7 provides a sample of the level of food stamps, AFDC, and medical assistance for the four counties of the LRGV. These figures underestimate the actual level of need since many of the poor fail to meet citizenship or other requirements imposed by government regulations.

More than one out of every four people in the LRGV lives outside an incorporated urban area. This makes meeting the needs of the poor particularly difficult. Within the region, Hidalgo county contains more than half the non-urban population, more than half the *colonia* population, and 70% of the *colonias* (see Chapter 3). The many service agencies in the county (and region) have established a wide range of programs in an attempt to alleviate the worst effects of poverty. To coordinate the efforts of these agencies, the Coalition of Community Service Agencies (CCSA) was formed in 1992. The CCSA has established four primary goals:

· to encourage the participation of the community in all aspects of the coalition
· to motivate the community to improve its standard of living through organization and education
· to create opportunities for networking and information sharing
· to coordinate and schedule coalition projects and events

TABLE 2.7

Texas Department of Human Services Statistics

	Cameron	Hidalgo	Starr	Willacy
Food Stamp Benefits				
(Jan-July 1992)				
# of Households	27,471 (37.5%)	44,312 (42.8%)	5,730 (55.5%)	1,974 (39.1%)
# of Persons	89,819 (34.5%)	146,556 (38.2%)	19,290 (47.6%)	6,708 (37.9%)
Stamp Value	$48,428,953	$85,559,872	$9,999,493	$3,204,457
AFDC				
(Jan-Sept.1992)				
# of Families	8,165 (22.7%)	12,965 (24.0%)	1,317 (21.0%)	503 (22.5%)
# of Children	16,573 (18.0%)	30,028 (21.4%)	4,014 (25.1%)	1,576 (24.3%)
Total Payments	$11,111,701	$ 2,079,355	$ 1,842,408	$ 695,385
Medical Assistance Program				
# of Cases				
(Sept.1992)	12,668	20,762	2,765	903
# of Recipients				
(Sept.1992)	18,053	31,711	4,050	1,334
Total Medical Exp.				
(Aug.1992)	$8,127,225	$10,191,541	$ 760,985	$ 236,489

Source: Information supplied by the Texas Department of Human Services.

To meet these goals, they have identified four broad, sometimes overlapping, areas of need: *colonia* housing and infrastructure, health care, employment and education, and human services.

Colonia Housing and Infrastructure

In the *colonias* which exist in rural areas, particularly in Hidalgo county, houses are typically built by the individual families who, in turn, live in them. The materials used are frequently scavenged from a variety of sources and do not meet standard building codes. They may lack heating, cooling, insulation, potable water, sewer lines, and electricity. Typically, they contain from one to four rooms, though they may house as many as fourteen people. Furniture and appliances are in limited supply in most of the homes and any electrical wiring which might exist often poses a fire hazard. Amenities such as smoke detectors and home insurance are rarely purchased by *colonia* residents.

Infrastructure problems include a lack of potable water lines and household connections. Few *colonias* have sewer connections or septic tanks. Only the newer *colonias* have paved roads and these usually lack curbs, proper drainage, street lights, or even street names. Many *colonias* also lack school bus service and for those that have bus service, few have sheltered bus stops for the students. The lack of utilities poses other problems as well. Most *colonias* have no phone service, garbage collection, or brush collection. Without street names or formal addresses, home mail delivery is impossible. Emergency medical service and fire protection is also hindered.

CCSA hopes to eliminate many of these problems. At present, several agencies in the coalition address infrastructure needs and *colonia* housing. The Hidalgo County Urban County Program distributes funds awarded by the Texas Department of Housing and Community Affairs for infrastructure in the *colonias*, particularly water and sewer facilities. BARCA, Inc. provides education and direct services on home maintenance and utilities. The Extension Home Economics (EHE) offers programs to help low income families learn about home safety, insurance, appliance selection and use, and home remodeling. Volunteer housing assistance to very low income families living in substandard housing is available from the Mission Service Project, while those families meeting HUD eligibility requirements can receive housing from the Pharr Housing Authority. Information to solve energy problems can be acquired from the Texas Energy Extension Service.

Health Care

Adequate health care is a pressing problem among the poor in the LRGV. The poor sanitation that characterizes the *colonias* leads to cholera and a wide range of intestinal disorders. Poor nutrition exacerbates the dental problems, hypertension, and the diabetes that exist. Children often rely on school breakfasts and lunches as their sole source of meals. These children are at risk in the summer when they fail to get enough to eat. Cancer, heart disease, high blood pressure, and mental illness pose long-term problems for those afflicted. Alcoholism and drug dependency, as well as the scourge of HIV/AIDS, have also found their way to the LRGV. Between November 1, 1989 and February 1, 1993, for example, the Valley Aids Council managed 266 cases of HIV/AIDS.[22]

The serious diseases found among the poor highlight the need for more health care resources. Both specialists and paraprofessionals are needed. Many of the poor who are ill lack transportation to seek the care they need. Those who have transportation complain about the long waits at public clinics, the high cost of medicine, and the lack of "after hours" care.

To avoid some of these problems, many of the poor cross the border and seek care and medicines in northern Mexico. Valley residents of all incomes have long known that expensive prescription drugs could be purchased inexpensively and over-the-counter in Mexico. Prenatal care is also needed to prevent many of the problems infants and mothers experience. Support groups would help the seriously ill and their families cope with the diseases they face.

A majority of the organizations in the CCSA address health care needs. As of 1993, for example, the Community Action Council Community Health Center administers a women, infants, and children program as well as primary health care services. The Texas Department of Health also offers a WIC program along with immunizations, health screenings, family planning, and treatment for sexually transmitted diseases. Border Health Projects is organizing specialty clinics to complement the primary health care it currently provides. Casa de la Merced, Comfort Care, Proyecto Salud, and the Valley Aids Council provide support and/or hospice care for AIDS victims or the terminally ill. Other groups focus on the elderly or mentally retarded and help arrange for transportation to and from medical facilities.

CCSA recognizes that health education would improve the quality of life for the poor in the LRGV. Nutrition, child development, basic safety, CPR, and the dangers of such things as pesticides and impure drinking water should be taught to the population, particularly the poor. Many of the organizations have developed programs dealing with these issues as well as others, including domestic violence and adolescent behavior problems.

Employment and Education

It is clear that lack of education and low skill levels contribute greatly to poverty in the LRGV. CCSA has identified a number of needs in this area and is working to improve the situation. For the very young, AVANCE, Project ARISE, and Su Casa de Esperanza provide early childhood education. Older children can receive tutoring and drop-out prevention services from Communities In Schools and Una Vida Mejor. H.E.P., the LaJoya ISD, and M.E.T. all help migrant workers improve their education. GED classes for all high school dropouts are conducted by the Coalition of Literacy Services, the Mission Service Project, and Region One ESC. English and literacy classes are taught through a number of different agencies.

Job training is another area that has been targeted by CCSA. The Department of Community Affairs and the Coalition of Literacy Services both currently offer job training. Outreach International also provides programs which help promote human development and self-sufficiency. More training and technical education is needed, however. Local community colleges and universities should work together with the technical institutes in northern Mexico to improve the job skill levels on both sides of the Rio Grande.

Human Services

Since many of the poor in the LRGV are foreign-born, they face a number of problems in dealing with the legal and cultural environment of their communities. Advocacy Inc., BARCA, and Texas Rural Legal Aid all help Valley residents with immigration information, legal services, civil rights, and availability of public benefits. Another problem is linked to the border drug trade, particularly in Starr County which is known as a haven for drug dealers. Like families throughout the country, Valley residents are concerned about drug dependency. Education programs in this area are provided by such organizations as the Mission Service Project, the Pharr Housing Authority, and the Tropical Texas Center for Mental Health and Mental Retardation. A great deal of effort is also taken to promote self-esteem among the Valley teens, in part to stem the rising incidence of gangs and teen pregnancy.

CCSA hopes to continue providing the poor with the education they need in the human services area. They want to increase the political awareness of the poor and help them achieve a degree of self-sufficiency. Their job has been made difficult by an unwillingness by those in need to accept or seek services. Some of this unwillingness is the result of inadequate information. Some comes from the tendency of the Valley poor to rely on their strong family networks to solve any problems that arise. And some stems from pride -- a determination to create a better world for their families without help from "outsiders." The poor of the LRGV are typically hardworking. They dream of a better life for themselves and especially for their children. Despite their pride, their hopes, and their dreams, they remain isolated and unable to integrate themselves fully into the economic mainstream.

2.8 The Efficacy of Public Policy

It should be evident that the antipoverty programs for the poor are expensive. Exact measurement is difficult because many programs serve the nonpoor as well as the poor. In 1977 the federal government spent about $1,500 per poor person. State, local, and philanthropic expenditures raised the figure by about 50%. Despite increased rhetorical emphasis on cash assistance, in-kind aid continued to expand in the 1970s, accounting for more than half of the federal outlays. By 1989, federal grants for public assistance (AFDC, SSI, food stamps, housing assistance, and nutrition programs) totaled $79.9 billion. These costs constituted 7% of the total federal budget, but they were only 1.5% of the total 1989 gross national product.[23] In December, 1992, 10.4% of the population (26.6 million people) received food stamp assistance. This represents the highest percentage of the population since the program began in 1964. Of this total, 2,645,900 were Texans.[24] No generally accepted agreement exists about what percentage of gross national product or even of governmental expenditures should be allocated to the poor. The experience in other countries is not of much help, because needs and programs differ widely among countries. As is evident from Table 2.6, welfare support varies greatly across nations. The U.S. is by no means at the top of rankings in battling the problem. Why this is so is not easily explained. In the final analysis, however, the level of expenditures probably depends on how strongly the public feels about the existence of poverty in an affluent society.

A 1990 study provided time series evidence on the correlation between federal income programs and the level of poverty.[25] Although this study did not test for feedback solely from poverty on specific programs, they did find feedback from employment programs when poverty was considered as one of the variables in a simultaneous equation system (a joint testing environment). This result is easily explained by the historical relation between these expenditures and the business cycle. It was argued that the relationship could be explained as a cost minimizing strategy by policymakers attempting to get a program through Congress and knowing their chances increase when public awareness of poverty is high and the program has some poverty reduction implications. The authors concluded that expenditures on these programs do not lead to more less poverty based on their testing schema. Indirect effects of specific programs on poverty over time do not seem to be significant.

The programs do seem to react to the poverty rate, however, which suggests that policy actions to deal with poverty are acting more as automatic stabilizers than as intended poverty reduction instruments. In other words, it does not appear that these poverty reduction instruments have been utilized with a steadfast intent to reduce poverty. Evidence suggests that the level of logrolling by special interest groups is substantial, a result that should not be surprising. Does society become too easily satisfied with modest reductions in poverty? Is it piqued only by media reported increases in poverty? In sum, what insight can be provided to the question, "Why is poverty so persistent?" The results of this study indicate that government's agenda is not served by a redistribution to the poor, except perhaps as a secondary effect -- a theorem proposed in an earlier work on poverty.[26]

While the federal government defines the official poverty threshold, each state sets its own basic needs standard for families without income. Historically, Texas has not been willing to pay 4-person families dollar amounts equal to those standards. This does not imply, however, that Texas ignores the needs of the poor. In 1990, Cameron, Hidalgo, Starr, and Willacy counties received $73.8 million, $124.4 million, $16.0 million, and $6 million respectively in federal grants for the following poverty eradication programs: AFDC, Food Stamps, Food Services and Nursing Homes. In 1990, 225,859 persons, or about 32.2% of the population of these counties combined, received food stamps valued at $159.4 million. This was an increase of 2% over the amount allocated in 1989. The food stamp program benefitted 72,936 people in Cameron County, 129,023 people in Hidalgo county, 17,378 in Starr county, and 6,522 monthly participants in Willacy county, with an average value of $58. This allotment allowed them to purchase necessary items in retail grocery stores. The number of LRGV recipients in the AFDC program in 1990 was 47,240 or about 6.7% of the population in the area; the cost of the program was $30.1 million. The AFDC program provided an average monthly payment of $54 to 16,742 people in Cameron county, to 26,778 people in Hidalgo county, to 2,495 people in Starr county, and to 1,225 recipients in Willacy county.[27]

Table 2.7 shows similar figures for 1992. The number of individuals and families receiving help from the Texas Department of Human Services had grown considerably in just two years. Yet, when one considers that 45% of the total population of the LRGV is considered poor, it is clear that many who need help are not receiving it. AFDC families in the LRGV received an average monthly payment of $173 in 1992, or $2076 annually for each family. Such cash income assistance does not come even close to the $12,675 poverty threshold. This makes the services of groups such as CCSA even more important if the needs of the poor are to be addressed at all.

2.9 Disincentive Implications of Public Policy

Whatever the mix of cash and non-cash benefits, many argue that the total welfare package throughout the U.S. is structured so that it carries with it strong disincentive effects for recipients to work. To a large degree, this is inevitable in any income transfer program. We presumably give aid to poor people because they are poor. If they become less poor, it makes sense to give them less aid. But that means that when a welfare recipient gets a job, and thus becomes less poor, we take some aid away. That, in effect, reduces the gain made from working.

Suppose a woman with two young children living in the LRGV has a part-time job and earns $400 per month. Her income will be supplemented with AFDC payments, food stamps, rent subsidies, and Medicaid. Now suppose she increases her work effort and raises her earned income to $500 per month. The result will be that her AFDC payment will be reduced by $67. Her food stamp allotment, rent subsidy, and Medicaid will fall. She will have to pay Social Security taxes on her additional income. Her earned income credit on her income tax will fall. The net result of all this will be a reduction in her total spendable income. Working harder will make her worse off -- and she will have to pay more for child care besides!

Efforts must be made to restore incentives. The Clinton administration has pledged to do this. Economists have long been enthusiastic about a plan suggested by Milton Friedman for a kind of "negative income tax." The plan would guarantee a basic income to all Americans. For each dollar an individual earned, he or she would be able to keep a certain fraction of it -- say 50%. Individuals would thus have a greater incentive to earn additional income than is the case with present welfare systems.

Another plan is the "negative wage tax." This scheme would first abolish the minimum wage law. It would then set a "benchmark" wage -- say, $8 an hour. People would find work at whatever the market would pay, and the government would supplement their wage by half the difference between their wage and the benchmark. With an $8 benchmark, for example, an individual who earned $1 an hour would get a supplement of an added $3.50 (half the difference between the wage and the benchmark). That person's total wage would thus be $4.50. People with wages greater than the benchmark would not, of course, get the supplement. The plan would expand incentives to work, particularly for handicapped workers who might be able to command only a very low wage in the market. The current economic situation in the LRGV suggests that such a program might have a significant impact if there is a concomitant increase in the demand for labor in the region. The North American Free Trade Agreement and the maquiladora industry obviously will play a pivotal role here.

2.10 Conclusion

Two key welfare reforms of the Reagan years -- the welfare eligibility restrictions of the 1981 Omnibus Budget Reconciliation Act (OBRA) and the creation of the Job Training Partnership Act in 1982 -- show why many government proposals may promise more than they can deliver. Both of those reforms also seemed surefire ways to slash the welfare rolls, yet each ended up having little or no practical effect, as we noted in observing the 1990 poverty rate of nearly 18% for the entire state of Texas.

To date, administration officials have essentially pursued two approaches to reforming job programs. They sought first to correct the abuses of previous job-training programs. Then, they created their own programs to try to show how it should be done. Correcting perceived abuses led to eliminating funding for the Comprehensive Employment and Training Act (CETA), the main program of job training and placement for welfare recipients. The Work Incentive Program (WIN) was reduced from $365 million in 1981 to $110 million in 1987, moving 130,000 people off welfare in 1985, or about one percent of those on AFDC.

Another program developed by the Reagan administration was the Job Training Partnership Act (JTPA), which established a program emphasizing quick placement in the private sector by teaching enrollees job search techniques and offering them short term training. But the Reagan administration never evaluated how similarly-situated welfare recipients who did not go through the JTPA program fared in finding work so it is unclear just how effective the program was or is.

During the 1980s, the Reagan/Bush administration touted Enterprise Zones to foster economic initiatives in urban areas in an attempt to eliminate poverty. President Clinton has announced he, too, will pursue Enterprise Zones. This particular program attempts to attract private businesses into depressed areas by promising tax breaks and fewer regulations. A recent NBER study analyzed Indiana's enterprise zone program, finding that less than 15% of jobs created were actually held by zone residents. The government's annual cost per new zone resident job was $31,113 while new zone residents earned an average of $11,746.[28] Apart from the inherent flaws in the proposal, it is not clear that such a project would benefit the LRGV. As we have seen, much of the poverty that exists in this area is rural and therefore would not be included in any proposal that targeted urban areas.

It is far from conclusive how we as a society can resolve the problems of social and economic inequality given domestic problems such as the budget deficit and the general disinclination of the capable public to expand programs for the poor. As we noted above, the relative isolation of the LRGV will certainly not serve to increase the desire to aid the destitute in this region. Most policy alternatives are considered too expensive to be considered at this time. Changing the current system would create costs to society that may be deemed socially undesirable, and expanding the system, as mentioned above, is presently unaffordable. The decisions for reform should be made after carefully weighing all costs and benefits at the margin.   Even then, it still would be difficult to implement any policies at a cost the public would find acceptable.

Regardless of how one calculates poverty, it is evident that widespread poverty is a problem in the LRGV.   It is also clear that alleviating such poverty is no simple task.   The remainder of this study examines the various economic development strategies to solve the problems posed by the substandard *colonias*, the growth of the maquiladora industry, the influx of population from Mexico, and the costs and benefits of the North American Free Trade Agreement.

Notes

1. See U.S. Bureau of the Census. *Characteristics of the Poor. Current Population Reports, Series P-60, No. 106* (Washington, D.C.: Government Printing Office, 1990).
2. M. Harrington. *The Other America: Poverty in the United States.* (New York: Penguin Books, 1981), p. 189.
3. M. Harrington. *The New American Poverty.* (New York: Penguin Books, 1984), p. 75.
4. M. Harrington. *The Other America.*, p. x.
5. A. Hagenaars and K. de Vos. "The Definition and Measurement of Poverty." *Journal of Human Resources*, Vol. 23 (1988): p. 211.
6. *Ibid.*, p. 213.
7. See I. Sawhill. "Poverty in the U.S.:Why Is It So Persistent?" *Journal of Economic Literature*, 26 (1988): 1073-1119.
8. *Ibid.*
9. See N. Birdsall. "A Cost of Siblings: Child Schooling in Urban Colombia." In *Research in Population Economics*, 2 (1980): 115-150.
10. K. Hayes, M. Nieswiadomy, and D. Slottje. "Multivariate Exogeneity Tests and Poverty." *Economic Letters*, 33 (1990): 395-399.
11. J. Eatwell, M. Milgate, and P. Newman, eds. *The New Palgrave Dictionary of Economics, Vol. 3* (New York: The Macmillan Press Ltd., 1987): p. 931.
12. 1990 Mexican Census of Population, State of Tamaulipas.
13. The fact that minimum wages and income in northeastern Mexico's border cities are high relative to the rest of the country encourages migration from the interior of Mexico. In the maquiladora industry total payments (including benefits) received by workers are three times greater than the national minimum wage. But the fact that wages are lower than those in the United States continues to encourage commuting and migration, both legally and illegally, across the border.
14. Mexico is expected to achieve relatively high rates of economic growth in the not-too-distant future. The annual growth rate for the first reporting period of 1991 registered growth in GDP at nearly 5% per year while inflation was down from 160% in 1987 to 18.8% in 1991.
15. E. Stoddard and J. Hedderson. *Trends and Patterns of Poverty Along the U.S. Mexico Border.* Borderlands Research Monograph Series, No. 3 (March 1987), p. 4.

16. See V. Loe. "Beyond City Limits." *The Dallas Morning News* (Sunday, February 28, 1993), pp. 22-23.

17. Bureau of the Census. *Statistical Abstract of the United States* (Washington, D.C.: Government Printing Office, 1991), p. 465.

18. S. Lee. "From Valley to New Peaks?" *The Dallas Morning News* (Monday, January 4, 1993), 1D.

19. S. Marquez. "Presidential Promises: What Will Clinton Do For Hispanics?" *Hispanic* (Jan./Feb. 1993): 23-28.

20. See *Texas Almanac, 1992-93*.

21. See S. Danzinger, R. Haveman, and R. Plotnick. "How Income Transfers Affect Work, Savings, and the Income Distribution." *Journal of Economic Literature*, 99 (1981): 975-1028.

22. Information obtained from the Valley Aids Council, February, 1993.

23. *Statistical Abstract of the United States*, 1991, p. 315.

24. "Number of people receiving food stamps hits record high." *Dallas Morning News* (Tuesday, March 2, 1993), p.3.

25. See Hayes, et al.

26. See G. Tullock. *The Economics of Wealth and Poverty*. (Boston: Kluwer, 1986).

27. Office of Strategic Management, Research, and Development. *1990 Annual Report* (Austin: Texas Department of Human Services, 1990).

28. See L. Papke. "Tax Policy and Urban Development: Evidence from an Enterprise Zone Program." NBER Working Paper No. 3945 (Cambridge: National Bureau of Economic Research, 1992).

Appendix: Coalition of Community Service Agencies

Adult Protective Services
2501 Maple St.
McAllen, TX 78501

Maintains a 24-hour, toll-free hotline to receive reports of abuse, neglect, or exploitation of elderly or disabled adults. Literature and speakers are available upon request.

Advocacy, Incorporated
225 South Cage St.
Pharr, TX 78577

A nonprofit corporation funded by the U.S. Congress to protect and advocate for the legal rights of persons with disabilities in Texas. It is funded under three separate federal laws to protect the legal rights of persons with developmental disabilities, persons with mental illness, and persons who are or have applied to be clients of the state vocational rehabilitation system. Advocacy, Inc. is completely separate from state or local government and is staffed by attorneys, paralegals, social workers, psychologists, rehabilitation specialists, and other professionals.

AVANCE - Rio Grande Valley
600 S. Bicentennial
McAllen, TX 78501

Offers a comprehensive parenting program to high risk families. The program includes parent education classes using a bilingual parenting curriculum and toymaking curriculum developed by AVANCE and an early childhood education program for children under 3 years of age. Others services include transportation to the center and a literacy program. As the program grows, additional components will include a Fatherhood program, after school tutoring for siblings, health services, college education, job training, and economic development.

BARCA, INC.
1701 N. 8th. St., Suite B-28
McAllen, TX 78501

Provides immigration information, legal workshops on immigration law, and helps process the necessary paperwork for legal residency, etc. BARCA, INC. also arranges community education and direct service programs in colonias on such issues as home maintenance, health, utilities, and school issues. It helps organize self-advocacy and direct action efforts toward *colonia* improvement.

Border Health Projects
6801 N. 15th St.
McAllen, TX 78577

Provides primary health care, health education, and mobile clinics to select colonias. BHP also trains health providers in cross cultural medicine and introduces high school students to health services careers.

Casa de la Merced
Rt. 2, Box 1680
McAllen, TX 78504

Serves as a support group for persons with HIV or AIDS, their families, and friends. Care, compassion, and support is provided along with speakers and programs of interest to persons with AIDS. Hot meals are available along with referrals for other services needed.

Coalition of Literacy Services, Inc.
700 Jackson Ave., #174
McAllen, TX 78501

Sponsors GED classes and volunteer reading, writing, and spelling classes for adults who need extra help. It also provides referrals for GED testing, free adult vocational classes, migrant GED classes, AFDC GED classes, free high school diploma night classes, and job skills training.

Comfort House
617 Dallas St.
McAllen, TX 78501

Provides 24-hour care for the terminally ill. Physical care, meals, palliative care, and companionship are among the services offered.

Community Action Council of South Texas
Community Health Centers
510 E. Eisenhower St.
Rio Grande City, TX 78582

Provides primary care health services, dental services, family planning, podiatry, WIC programs, health education, and environmental services.

Communities In Schools - McAllen, Inc.
801 South Main St.
McAllen, TX 78501

Provides comprehensive drop out prevention services to include: counseling, tutoring, enrichment activities, and parental involvement.

Department of Community Affairs
Hidalgo County
1899 N. Cage St.
Pharr, TX 78577

Provides training and placement services for any disadvantaged person 14 years of age or older living in Hidalgo or Willacy county.

Elderconnection Case Management Program
4900 N. 23rd St.
McAllen, TX 78501

Provides case management services which include individual assessment, service plan development, arrangement of services, follow-up, ongoing monitoring, and periodic revision of the service plan. Service plans include emergency response, medical transportation, health maintenance, home modifications, home health services, home delivered meals, and emergency shelter.

Extension Home Economics
District Extension Office
Weslaco, TX 78596

Provides opportunities for strengthening families and individuals through education in the following areas: family life education, health education, consumer education, resource management, housing and home furnishings, food and nutrition, and extension leadership.

Food Bank of the Rio Grande Valley, Inc.
2601 Zinnia
McAllen, TX 78501

Serves families who fail to qualify for state and federal assistance programs and people who have emergency situations.

H.E.P. (High School Equivalency Program)
University of Texas Pan American
1201 W. University Drive
Edinburg, TX 78539

Helps prepare seasonal farmworkers and migrant workers for the GED.

Hidalgo County Health Department
1015 S. 10th
Edinburg, TX 78539

Provides health inspections and animal and bee control to endure safe water supplies and prevent diseases.

Hidalgo County Human Services
1304-B S. 25th Street
Edinburg, TX 78539

Provides assistance with funeral expenses, transportation to and from medical facilities outside the Valley area, assistance with ambulance service, and assistance with such medical expenses as hospital services, physician services, prescription drugs, lab and x-ray services, family planning services, and skilled nursing home care.

Hidalgo County Urban County Program
100 E. Cano, 2nd Floor
Edinburg, TX 78539

Granter of CDBG funds that are used for community development. The program administers monies for infrastructure in the colonias and solicits and encourages input from the public on prospective colonias that are in need of infrastructure.

Horizons of Mission
405 W. 12th St.
Mission, TX 78572

Sponsors parenting sessions, the Amigo/Mentor program, the Juvenile Court Conference Committee, Teen's Own Print Shop, and peer counseling. Teatro, a group which uses acting to focus on the problems of youth, and WINGS, a Saturday activity group with youth ministers from area churches, are also sponsored by Horizons.

Housing Authority of the City of Mission
906 East 8th St.
Mission, TX 78572

Provides low income housing to those residents over 18 who qualify.

International Eye Care
301 N. Main St.
McAllen, TX 78501

Supplies a vision program, as well as glucose and cholesterol testing.

La Joya ISD
P.O. Drawer J
La Joya, TX 78560

Provides parenting sessions, migrant education, and promotes parental involvement.

Lutheran Social Service of Texas, Inc. Guardianship Program
1420 Erie St.
McAllen, TX 78504

Provides guardianship services through a professional staff member. The agency as a corporation is named the actual legal guardian with a staff person responsible for carrying out the duties and responsibilities required of the guardian.

Mission Service Project
405 West 12th St.
Mission, TX 78572

Provides volunteer housing assistance to very low income families living in substandard housing. Self Help Housing Assistance gives low income families to opportunity to build their own new home by being able to work at a construction site for 46 weeks while getting paid minimum wages. Recipients attend classes to learn English, take GED classes, parenting classes, and drug awareness classes.

Motivation Education & Training, Inc
154 N. Texas St.
Weslaco, TX 78596

Provides services to migrant and other seasonal farmworkers. These services include on-the-job training, classroom training, and work experience. MET also offers trainee financial aid and a variety of supportive services to assure completion of training and retention of permanent employment.

Mujeres Unidas
420 N. 21st St.
McAllen, TX 78501

Provides shelter for abused women and children, legal advocacy for victims of domestic violence, crisis counseling for sexual assault victims, accompaniment to hospital, court, and police station, and a Men Against Violence Program for men who want to change abusive behavior.

Office of the Attorney General
3201 N. McColl Rd.
McAllen, TX 78501

Provides complaint mediation, investigation of deceptive trade practices, speakers on consumer topics, and pamphlets on consumer information.

Outreach International
2220 N. Bryan Rd.
McAllen, TX 78502

Supports and participates in the creation and replication of comprehensive programs for human development among the poor. Programs mobilize volunteer, financial, professional, and technical resources to facilitate development. OUTREACH involves local people as partners in the planning and implementation of programs designed to improve health, education, livelihood, and community organization.

P.A.T.H. Project
P.O. Box 3700
McAllen, TX 78502

Provides services to parents of infants, toddlers, children, and youth with all types of disabilities. Services include training, information, referral, resources, consultation, and emotional support. Workshops are provided on parenting a child with special needs, educational rights, assertiveness and communication, record keeping and case management, and parent/professional partnerships.

Pharr Housing Authority
211 W. Audrey St.
Pharr, TX 78577

Provides sanitary, safe, decent housing to families and elderly that meet eligibility requirements. Additional programs promote self-sufficiency among participating families and provides prevention, intervention, referral, treatment, and aftercare for residents.

Planned Parenthood
1017 Pecan
McAllen, TX 78501

Provides services in three areas: medical services (HIV testing, daily family planning, pregnancy testing, sexually transmitted diseases), routine services (blood pressure, breast examination, contraception, pap smears, pelvic exams, urinalysis, weight control), counseling (AIDS/HIV, infertility, pregnancy, tubal ligation, vasectomy), referrals (adoption, infertility, pregnancy termination, prenatal care, sterilization), and educational services (A.C.T.T., AIDS, family planning, parent/child workshops, sexual abuse prevention, family life programs).

Project ARISE
125 E. Denny Dr.
Pharr, TX 78577

Empowers the people of Las Milpas to become functional productive members of society. Provides the following services: English classes, pre-school readiness, Ballet Folkloric classes for children, guitar lessons for children, storytelling sessions, parenting skills, and personal development.

Proyecto Salud
Rt. 2 Box 1680
McAllen, TX 78504

Provides creative, informative presentations on HIV/AIDS in the form of "outreach" activities, public service announcements, brochures, and posters. The group sponsors a Women's Advisory Board for HIV/AIDS, a support group for persons with HIV, and intensive workshops.

Region One ESC
2500 Quince St.
McAllen, TX 78501

Offers the following services to legal residents: ESL, GED, ABE, and other instructional services.

Rio Transit Express
4900 N. 23rd St.
McAllen, TX 78501

Transfers customers to and from physicians' offices, pharmacies, hospitals, and other medical facilities on a non-emergency basis.

Su Casa de Esperanza, Inc.
P.O. Box 1333
Pharr, TX 78577

Provides the following services for expectant parents: care for mothers, home visits to mothers with infants, monthly parenthood classes and support groups, assistance in finding information and services, and group meetings with toddlers.

Texas Department of Health
601 W.Sesame Drive
Harlingen, TX 78550

Provides services in the following areas: adult health, child health, immunization, maternal health, tuberculosis control, Hansen's disease, sexually transmitted diseases, chronically ill and disabled children, family planning, dental health, women, infants, and children (WIC), vision, hearing, and speech, emergency medical services, long term care, cooperative meat inspection, zoonosis control, environmental and consumer health protective services, indigent health care, primary care services and manpower placement program.

Texas Department of Human Services
600 S. Bicentennial
McAllen, TX 78501

Provides AFDC, Medicaid, and food stamps to McAllen clients.

Texas Department of Human Services
2520 N. Closner
Edinburg, TX 78539

Provides primary home care services, family care services, home delivered meals, emergency response service, day activity and health services, and adult foster care for aged and disabled Hidalgo county residents.

Texas Energy Extension Service
University of Texas - Pan American
1201 W. University Drive
Edinburg, TX 78539

Assist Texans in the efficient and cost-effective use of energy in their homes and small businesses. TEES offers a wide range of services, including publications, educational programs, personalized answers to specific questions from energy consumers, an energy information Hotline, and an audio-visual lending library.

Texas Rural Legal Aid, Inc.
259 S. Texas Blvd.
Weslaco, TX 78596

Provides help with all types of cases: employment, civil rights, public benefits, housing, consumer problems, education, and health care.

Tip of Texas Girl Scouts
500 Indiana St.
Weslaco, TX 78596

Works to extend Girl Scouting to underprivileged areas in the LRGV. The group develops programs that will communicate family values to girls, to help underprivileged girls become a part of the greater community, and to recruit adult volunteers to foster leadership skills, communications skills, and basic business administration skills.

Tropical Texas Center for Mental Health and Mental Retardation
1901 S. 24th St.
Edinburg, TX 78539

Provides help for the mentally retarded, screens and refers clients, and sponsors substance abuse services.

University of Texas, Hidalgo County Mobile Clinic
1304 S. 25th St.
Edinburg, TX 78539

Provides examinations for children, vaccinations, examinations for breast cancer, pregnancy, and pap smears, checks for anemia, and provides blood pressure exams for men and women. It also offers education and assistance in nutrition, diets for cholesterol and diabetes, and nutrition during pregnancy.

Una Vida Mejor
410 N. 13th Street
Edinburg, TX 78540

Provides educational programs in select colonias to meet community needs, help children succeed in school, help with crime prevention, and promote parenting skills.

Valley AIDS Council
2220 Haine Drive, Suite 33
Harlingen, TX 78550

Provides case management, HIV Counseling and Testing, client/family education, dental services, home hospice care, food pantry, transportation, and housing assistance.

Valley Information Project
1235 E. Jefferson St.
Brownsville, TX 78520
834 E. Citrus, St.
Alamo, TX 78516

A food stamp demonstration project with a goal to increase participation by eligible low-income households in the Food Stamp Program. This project also tries to determine barriers people encounter in accessing DHS services (transportation, illiteracy, fear of INS deportation).

3

Colonias and Economic Development

3.1 Introduction

Poverty more acute than that of Appalachia can be found in the *colonias* that dot the countryside of the LRGV. The term "colonia" has been officially defined as a poor, rural unincorporated community with 20 or more dwelling units where home ownership is the norm.[1] These communities are characterized by one or more of the following conditions: substandard housing, inadequate roads and drainage, and substandard or total lack of water and sewer facilities. Clearly, they differ from city neighborhoods, but variation exists among the individual *colonias* as well.

Early *colonias* consisted of small communities of farm workers who worked for a single employer. Between 1908 and 1948 realtors started unincorporated townships which now comprise less than one-fifth of the *colonias*. Most of these communities have sprung up since the early 1960s when land developers sold small plots of land in unincorporated subdivisions to low-income people. For the poor who dreamed of owning their own home, the low downpayment and monthly payments were attractive. Lots could be purchased for as little as $10 down and $25 per month. Often, no costs were incurred for installation of water, sewer, and gas lines since none were provided. Texas law merely required the developers to provide roads and drainage.

Even in recent years a typical lot of about 50 feet by 100 feet has sold for $2000 to $8000. The developer frequently provides financing under a "contract for sale" arrangement, usually without a deed of ownership accompanying the sale. For the buyer, this has meant that there is no buildup of equity. For the seller (the developer), the property and any improvements can be foreclosed on if a payment is missed. Such a practice places the largest amount of risk on those least able to afford it.[2]

Once lots had been purchased, owners could then build their own home. Many chose (and choose) to live in trailers and uncompleted

67

homes while construction took place. No zoning codes were in effect since *colonias* are located in rural areas. The roads provided were often ungraded dirt roads that became a sea of mud during the rains that sometimes drenched the area.

Other considerations have also prompted people to live in *colonias*. Many were attracted to the rural life which they felt would be less expensive than an urban life with high property taxes, zoning ordinances, and building codes. Many came to live near relatives. One survey found that 80% of household heads had relatives living in the same *colonia*.[3] Family is extremely important to many *colonia* residents. For most, however, the otherwise unattainable ability to own a home attracted them to the *colonias*. Nearly 87% of the residents do own, rather than rent, their homes.[4]

Living conditions in the *colonias*, however, belie the American dream. Twelve hundred interviews of *colonia* residents collected by the Texas Department of Human Services found the following:[5]

- · 65% of *colonia* residents have no health insurance
- · 67% of those over 18 did not complete high school
- · unemployment is 41% among those over 16 who are not in school
- · 26% of households report inadequate heating
- · 24% of homes are not connected to treated water
- · 44% report that flooding is a problem in their *colonia*
- · 15% of households report they do not usually have enough to eat

Additional media reports have added chronic disease, overcrowded schools, high fertility rates, high infant mortality rates, and poor prenatal care to this list of problems. Testimony by experts in a wide range of areas in various public forums has supported this bleak portrait of a population at risk. It is for these reasons that the LRGV has been referred to as a "grim new Appalachia."[6]

3.2 *Colonias* in the LRGV

Colonias exist all along the U.S. border with Mexico from Texas to California. The worst of the squalor, however, occurs in the LRGV. Nearly 17% of the population of the four counties comprising the LRGV live in a total of 552 *colonias* and the numbers are increasing (see Table 3.1). Houses in the *colonias* are typically substandard, owner-built, wooden, single family dwellings consisting of two rooms plus bathroom and kitchen. Some are made of used cinder blocks with dirt floors and no

TABLE 3.1

County Summaries of *Colonias*, 1989

County	Colonia Population	# of Colonias	# with Water Systems	# with Sewer Systems
Cameron	44,931	115ᵃ	103	2
Hidalgo	60,000	366	329	0
Starr	10,000	62	9	0
Willacy	3,402	9	7	0
Total	118,333	552	448	2

ᵃ La Coma and Portway Acres, just outside Brownsville in Cameron county, are subdivisions that are considered *colonias* even though they have public water and sewer. They are considered *colonias* since they have substandard housing.

Source: U.S. General Accounting Office, *Rural Development: Problems and Progress of Colonia Subdivisions Near Mexico Border*, 1990.

insulation. Lots are small and streets are unpaved and poorly drained and lighted. Nearly all have electricity of some sort, though it may come via a bright orange extension cord plugged into an outside outlet. Less than 50% have telephones.[7] Green garden hoses stretch from an outside spigot across most of the lots.

These generally dismal communities grew because effective land-use controls were not in place.[8] Within the federal government, the Department of Transportation, the Department of Housing and Urban Development, the Environmental Protection Agency, and the Department of Interior all have some measure of land-use control. Jurisdiction in rural areas where *colonias* exist, however, has been left to state and local governments. At the state level, agencies coordinate special districts, control environmental pollution, and manage state lands. State law enables cities to regulate land development and utilization within city boundaries which exclude *colonias*. Other state control of land-use follows the pattern of the federal government and is delegated to local government bodies.

One of the local government bodies involved in land-use management consists of voluntary associations of local governments called regional councils of government. These councils assist local governments in solving problems affecting more than one jurisdiction, encourage the development of inter-governmental relations, review local planning activities, and maintain an areawide comprehensive planning process. Unfortunately, regional councils may only make recommendations. They do not have the power to enforce the recommendations.

County government, another local government body, does possess some land-use control. Developers of unincorporated land must file plats with the county clerk before subdividing land. Specifications for construction and drainage of roads and streets are established by the county. However, loopholes exist in the current statutes which allow the sale of lots in unapproved subdivisions. These unrecorded subdivisions have no access to city services since no official record of them exists. Many of the *colonia* fit into this category.

Yet another form of local government, municipal government, also has some land-use control. All Texas cities have the authority to implement zoning laws, building and housing codes, and subdivision ordinances within city limits. Some cities have authority in unincorporated areas which lie within their extra-terrestrial jurisdiction (ETJ) and consists of contiguous areas, not a part of another city, within a specified distance of the city limit. Specified distances vary from one-half mile to 5 miles. Subdivision ordinances may be imposed on unincorporated areas within a city's ETJ but no fines may be imposed for violations. Cities can only refuse to provide services to subdivisions which violate ordinances. Thus, under current land-use control, subdivisions like *colonias* are difficult to deal with. Any penalties tend to exacerbate an already serious problem.

Residents of *colonias* are typically Mexican-Americans who work as seasonal labor. Incomes for many are below the poverty level. Less than 82% have access to public water systems and almost none have approved sewer systems. Few homes have indoor plumbing and most typically use septic tanks and pit privies which do not meet public health standards.[9] When it rains, children who live in the *colonias* attend school in clothes stained with the mud and sewage they trudged through to come to class. The stagnant water they use and drink adds to the high rates of parasitic infection and chronic skin diseases.[10]

Representatives from Texas Rural Legal Aid, Inc. have examined water provision in a number of Texas *colonias* and have found four basic scenarios:[11]

- Many *colonias* simply have no access to water whatsoever. There are no pipes in the ground or wells. Water must be obtained by hauling

it from a relative who lives in a *colonia* with some form of water. Others haul water from irrigation ditches. The water in this case is contaminated with fecal material from livestock and with agricultural pesticides.
· Some *colonias* have individual wells dug by the residents. However, because the lots are so small, many of these wells are dug next to an outhouse so that serious fecal contamination occurs.
· Some communities actually have wells provided by the developer. In nearly every instance, however, the water does not meet Texas Health Department standards. Tests have found it heavily contaminated with high levels of fecal material and bacteria.
· In those communities with access to a water system, the water supply corporation either lacks the capacity to treat the quantity of water needed or fails to provide the appropriate pipes to actually distribute it to the homes that need it.

The Cameron County Community Development Coordinator has estimated that nearly 45,000 people live in 115 *colonias* in Cameron county (see Figure 3.1). Only two of these *colonias* have both sewage and water facilities while another 101 have water systems only. The remaining 12 have neither water nor sewer systems. Water is provided by a combination of five nonprofit water corporations and municipal water suppliers who have used Farmers' Home Administration (FmHA) loan and grant funds to extend water service to the area. Since Cameron is considered a rural county, federal Department of Housing and Urban Development (HUD) Community Block Development Grant (CBDG) funds are not available to provide assistance.

Hidalgo County contains the largest number of *colonias* in the LRGV. The Chief Planner has estimated that 366 *colonias* housing 60,000 people exist in the county (see Figure 3.2). These *colonias* have no sewage system, relying upon on-site sewage disposal. Four nonprofit water corporations supply the 329 *colonias* which have any form of water system. Many residents with access to water either rely on an outside water spigot for water or cannot afford to hook into the system at all. Because Hidalgo is considered to be an urban county, both CBDG and FmHA funds have been used to provide street improvements and to extend water systems.

The Starr County Coordinator of Federal and State Programs has listed 62 *colonias* with 10,000 residents (see Figure 3.3). None of these *colonias* have sewage systems and only 42 have access to water systems. These water systems are provided by public, nonprofit water supply corporations and the cities of Roma and La Gruilla. They are frequently plagued by inadequate water pressure. Those *colonias* without access to public water use well water that is often contaminated. Pit privies and substandard

72

FIGURE 3.1 - *Colonia* Locations in Cameron and Willacy Counties, 1990

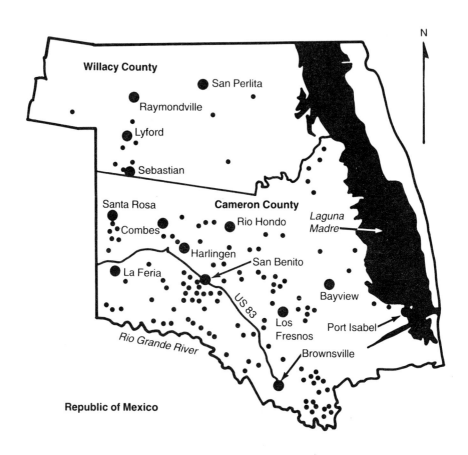

• *Colonia* Designation
● Cities or Towns

Source: General Accounting Office, *Rural Development: Problems and Progress of Colonia Subdivisions Near Mexico Border*, 1990.

FIGURE 3.2 - *Colonia* Locations in Hidalgo County, 1990

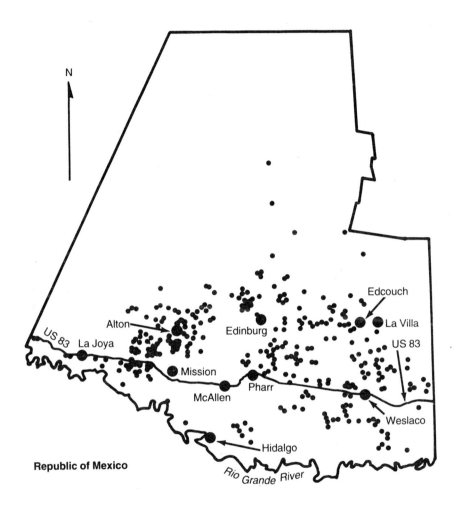

- *Colonia* Designation
- Cities or Towns

Source: General Accounting Office, *Rural Development: Problems and
Progress of Colonia Subdivisions Near Mexico Border*, 1990.

FIGURE 3.3 - *Colonia* Locations in Starr County, 1990

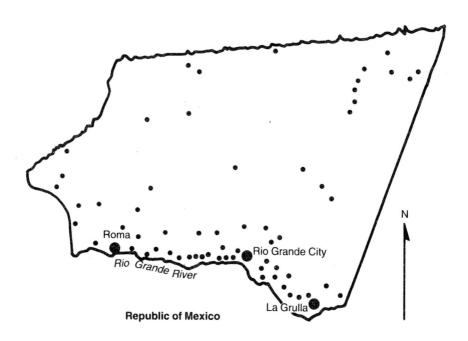

- *Colonia* Designation
- Cities or Towns

Source: General Accounting Office, *Rural Development: Problems and Progress of Colonia Subdivisions Near Mexico Border*, 1990.

septic tanks comprise the only sewage system available. The county has used FmHA funds to extend water lines and fund a water treatment facility.

Willacy county had only 9 *colonias* with 3,402 residents in 1990 (see Figure 3.1). Of these *colonias*, 7 had water systems while 2 did not. The city of Lyford and three nonprofit water supply corporations provide water for the *colonias*, though, like in Starr county, water pressure is often inadequate. In addition, many residents simply cannot afford the fees for a public water supply. Like the other counties, sewage facilities consist of pit privies and substandard septic tanks. As of 1990, no federal funds had been acquired to help alleviate the conditions in the county's *colonias*.

A detailed study of Cameron, Hidalgo, and Willacy counties found a number of problems with housing and infrastructure.[12] More than one-third of the households perceived their heating as inadequate and nearly 29% felt the same way about their cooling or ventilation. Water problems were especially acute. More than 21% of the households had no treated water in their homes. Of these, nearly 8% had a water outlet on the property while 14% had no treated water in the house or on the property. This forced as many as 7% of the households to use untreated water for many common activities, such as drinking, washing dishes, washing clothes, bathing, and cooking.

As mentioned above, only two of the colonias have sewer systems actually installed. This means households must rely on septic tanks, outhouses, and other pit privies. Nearly 60% of the households have septic tanks, though many of these are incorrectly installed and maintained. An additional 12% have outhouses. Cesspools and similar pits account for the remaining households. Such arrangements become more dangerous when flooding occurs. Households in more than 90% of the *colonias* have reported flooding at least once. Flooding has long been a serious problem in the region because of the flat terrain and poor overall drainage.

Most of the communities in the LRGV discharge their effluent into three highly polluted floodways: the Main Floodway, the North Floodway, and the Arroyo Colorado Floodway. These, in turn, drain into the Rio Grande River, making this segment of the river unsuitable for contact recreation. The poor-quality water is marked by low levels of dissolved oxygen, high fecal coliform counts, and high concentrations of suspended solids. Groundwater in the region is also contaminated with a high concentration of dissolved solids. *Colonias* typically discharge nearly 2 million gallons of waste water into sub-surface excavations per day. This waste water seeps into a water table that is already high and contributes to the heavy floods that regularly occur in the region. Flooding, in turn, pushes raw sewage on the surface of the land, creating a serious health problem.[13]

Septic tanks, the most common type of sewer system in the *colonias*, fail to solve the sewage problems in the region. In most *colonias*, population density is simply too high for septic tanks to be safe. Soil conditions in many cases are too poor to accommodate septic tanks. Also, the National Flood Insurance Act will not insure new homes with unsealed sewage facilities built in floodplains. For all these reasons, improved methods for waste disposal must be provided for the *colonias*.[14]

Securing appropriate waste treatment facilities for the *colonias* poses two particular problems. First, organizations must be created to install the systems. As noted above, *colonias* fall outside the jurisdiction of city services and most counties are ill-equipped to meet their needs. Second, funding must be secured for the installation. Estimates made a few years ago for Cameron and Hidalgo counties placed capital costs for the two combined at over $10 million. Average annual cost per household was over $200. These amounts are beyond the means of *colonia* residents whose incomes fall well below the poverty line.[15]

The groundwater pollution caused by inadequate sewage facilities also affects pollution in the floodways and the Rio Grande River, making it unsuitable for extensive irrigation. This means, too, that wells in the region typically violate standards set by the United States Public Health Service. Since many *colonia* residents lack access to public water supplies, they rely instead on water from shallow wells and irrigation ditches. Water, then, is the source of some of the problems that exist in the region.[16] Education about the effects of using unsafe water can help, but not eliminate the problem.

Attempts to solve the water problem have not been entirely successful. Most plans are expensive and cannot provide water immediately. The Center for Inter-American and Border Studies in El Paso proposed a novel threefold approach to the problem in 1989. Using cultural and economic conditions that exist in the *colonias*, this approach provided potable water, conserved the water, and disposed of waste water. The plan called for a water purifier based on ultraviolet radiation that would allow production of 10 gallons per minute of highly purified water at a cost of pennies per month. One unit would serve up to four families and cost between $100 and $300. Once potable water was available, residents would be shown how to conserve water with efficient plumbing devices. With conservation, the electrical costs of running the purifier would be lower and the area needed to treat dirty water would be limited. To treat waste water, the plan proposed to use a biological application to destroy organic fecal matter. The entire project could be assembled by the residents themselves, paid for by the week as construction took place. It would require no large upfront costs.[17] While a pilot program was implemented, little has been done to adapt this process for widespread use in *colonias*.

3.3 Socio-economic Characteristics of *Colonias*

More than 67% of the rural population of the LRGV live in *colonias* which are physically and legally isolated from neighboring cities. A 1988 study revealed that nearly 99% of this population was Hispanic, though 61% were born in the U.S.[18] However, less than 40% of the household heads were born in the U.S. The population of the *colonias* is young. The average age of a *colonia* resident is 18.5 years and more than 80% of them are actually 18 years old or younger. Spanish is the primary language for most of the residents. More than 40% can neither read nor write English. This is reflected in the low average annual household income of $6,784.

The low incomes of the residents aggravate the health problems that have become a concern, not only of those living in the *colonias*, but of local government officials as well. Third World diseases such as bacillary and amoebic dysentery, tuberculosis, typhoid, and viral hepatitis occur with frightening regularity. Most of these diseases are spread by water-borne fecal contamination. Almost three-fourths of the residents lack any form of health insurance which forces them to seek low-cost health care in Mexico. More than 60% of the *colonia* residents report traveling to Mexico to receive health care and 30% admit to having unpaid medical bills. Many mothers fail to receive adequate prenatal care, causing high infant mortality rates. Small children frequently die from preventable diseases because they do not receive the necessary inoculation. This occurs for a number of reasons: lack of information about such programs as WIC, the fear of expense, a lack of transportation, pride, and a lack of U.S. citizenship. Teenage pregnancies are also a problem. Nearly 40% of females between 14 and 19 years of age become pregnant.[19]

Lack of education poses another serious threat to the well-being of *colonia* residents. Nearly one-third of them never attend high school, while another 47% quit before graduation. For those who are heads of households, the figures are even more discouraging. Almost 40% of family heads have never attended high school. Of the less than 2% of high school graduates who go on to college, three out of four do not graduate. In testimony before the House of Representatives' Select Committee on Hunger in 1989, the late Hon. Mickey Leland argued:

Colonia children growing up in abject poverty must wonder what it is that society can offer them. For a student to achieve, self-esteem is necessary. It is difficult for those students who grow up in the *colonias* to have a positive attitude about themselves. They begin their education on a level that lags behind that of their counterparts who live in better environments. They are further disadvantaged by the poor facilities and services offered by the schools they attend. It is no wonder that the high school drop-out rate is as high as 40%. And in many cases, much higher than that. Both parents and educators have a difficult job attempting to convince these students that their lot in life does not have to duplicate the lifestyle they currently have. For those who manage to graduate from high school, opportunities still remain limited. With an average unemployment rate of 30%, people are forced to leave their communities and move to the larger cities in search of jobs.[20]

Vocational training, which could alleviate some of the problems caused by lack of education, has not been successfully utilized. Less than 12% of those over the age of 16 and not in school have received vocational training. This has contributed to unemployment rates of up to 47%. Higher unemployment rates exist for women. For those residents able to find employment, 46% work as field hands, 15% in construction, 11% in factories, and 7% each in retail sales and janitorial work. Almost half work for minimum wage or less.

Such poverty compels many of the *colonia* residents to seek help from the Department of Human Services. Below is a list of DHS services and the percentage of *colonia* households using those services in recent years.

Food Stamps - 56.6%
Aid to Families with Dependent Children - 9.8%
Medicaid - 20.7%
Home Energy Assistance Program - 20.7%
In-home Services for the Elderly - 1.7%
Family self-support - 3.3%
Children's Protective Services - 0.4%
Food Services - 63.7%
Family Violence Temporary Placement - 1.7%

Despite the fact that approximately 15% of the *colonia* households do not have enough to eat, 26% of them receive no food aid. Many households are simply not aware of the services available or are too proud to accept help.

3.4 Efforts to Address the Problems

No single entity can hope to address the myriad problems that exist in the *colonias*. Chapter Two outlined the efforts being made by local service organizations to deal with many of the more pressing problems. For infrastructure needs, it has been estimated that it would take 30 years and at least $200 million just to bring water and sewer lines to all the existing *colonias*.[21] The actual prevention of uncontrolled growth of *colonias* poses serious social concerns since *colonias* provide cheap housing for the poor as well as contribute to the health problems of the region. To simply eliminate the *colonias* would displace thousands of families and would be unacceptable. It would certainly be better to improve the existing *colonias* and prevent the creation of new ones. In this regard, a number of efforts have been made in recent years.

At the federal level, Congressmen from the *colonia* districts have proposed several legislative initiatives in an attempt to address the problems. These include:

· A bill to enhance the prospects in rural areas by allowing municipal corporations to acquire through eminent domain utility facilities of rural water supply or sewer service corporations;

· A bill to provide grants and loans to enable rural areas near the international border separating the United States and Mexico to develop plans for the coordination and improvement of, and to construct and improve, water and waste water disposal facilities;

· A bill to establish the United States - Mexico Border Regional Commission and to assist in the development of the economic and human resources of the United States - Mexico border region of the United States;

· A bill to direct the Administrator of the Environmental Protection Agency to establish a demonstration program for installation of sewer and water supply facilities for certain *colonias* in the state of Texas and to establish a revolving loan fund to enable residents of such *colonias* to connect their residences to such facilities, and for other purposes.

Because of budget constraints and bureaucratic inertia, Congress has been unwilling to take drastic measures to improve conditions in *colonias*.

Federal help has been forthcoming, however, in the form of grants from funding agencies of the government to be used in financing water or waste water systems development. The U.S. Department of Agriculture's Farmers Home Administration (FmHA) has supplied grants and loans to eight nonprofit water supply corporations providing service to the LRGV counties. In addition, a number of cities and districts in the LRGV have received Community Development Block Grants from the U.S. Department of Housing and Urban Development, grants from the Economic Development Administration, and construction grants from the Environmental Protection Agency. Between 1978 and 1987, these funds totaled more than $79 million.[22]

At the state level, the Texas Water Development Board has attempted to address the water supply and sewer needs of the *colonias*. Studies were conducted on the counties of the LRGV to identify the size, location, and population of the *colonias*; to determine existing water and sewer arrangements; to project water and sewer service needs through the year 2010; and to identify and estimate costs of various solutions to the problems. The Board has also been active in helping the counties secure grants for regional planning. It has provided loans at the lowest possible rates to cities and districts, enabling them to supply water and waste water services to *colonias*. As a part of their efforts, the Board issued the following recommendations:[23]

· Future waste water planning should include both the *colonia* and *non-colonia* rural developments in the LRGV;
· The full participation of the residents in the *colonias* will be a factor in the financial and operational success of water/waste water facilities. Incentive programs to ensure participation should be implemented;
· Use of Innovative/Alternative (I/A) systems for waste water management should be considered. A demonstration program at selected *colonias* incorporating these I/A systems should be implemented as a means of developing a data base on cost, maintenance, and management requirements;
· A single management organization should be implemented to consolidate the professional expertise necessary to finance and maintain the overall waste water system;
· Detailed analysis of the individual *colonias* may be required prior to selecting specific methods for any individual *colonia* or group of *colonias*.

Legislation was passed in Texas in 1989 requiring rural subdivisions to adopt rules mandating the adequate provision of drinking water and sewer facilities. The rules adopted must prohibit construction of more than one single-family detached dwelling per tract. Under the legislation, residential developments include individual tracts of 1 acre or less. Some concern exists that developers could circumvent the legislation by creating subdivision tracts larger than 1 acre.[24]

The 1989 legislation also amended the State Water Code to provide financial assistance to water supply and sewage disposal projects. This has since become a state constitutional amendment with $100 million in bonds authorized for the loans and grants to economically distressed counties and to all border counties containing *colonias*. Three additional funds to be administered by the Texas Water Development Board have also been set up to assist eligible rural subdivision water and/or waste water projects: the Texas Water Development Fund, the Water Assistance Fund, and the State Revolving Fund. Only those subdivisions which meet the model rules mentioned above are eligible for financial assistance from these funds.[25]

Funding options typically available for water and waste water systems in the state include:[26]

- Texas Department of Community Affairs (TDCA) Community Development Program Regular Fund - This is a regional competition among small cities and counties. It is a non-entitlement program since federal monies can be used only if the population is 50,000 or less.
- TDCA Special Impact Fund - This is available as grants awarded in a statewide competition. This fund is strictly for counties and is designed to assist substandard subdivisions in the unincorporated areas of the county. These monies may not be used for housing-related activities, but can be used for street and drainage improvements, and water and sewer improvements.
- TDCA Areawide Revitalization Fund - This fund provides grants in statewide competition for small cities and counties. The focus here is on housing-related activities.
- Farmers Home Administration Rural Water Supply Loans or Grants - Rural water supply companies can apply for these funds. Partial grants are needed to reduce the loan amount, which in turn, reduces the repayment burden on water and sewer customers.
- Municipal Utility Districts - These may be considered for individual *colonias* of substantial size. Taxing and bond issuing capabilities would provide revenue for infrastructure improvements.
- Environmental Protection Agency (EPA) - Construction grants may be available to cities and utilities to provide waste water treatment and collection for *colonias*. Location of industrial growth in strategic areas could offset the cost of extending water and sewer lines. EPA public works grants would reduce the overall costs here.
- Community and Health Service Organizations - Organizations that are possible sources of funding for grants or no-interest loans for hook-up fees and home improvement efforts include private foundations, health and human services administration, and community services administration.

Texas Rural Aid, Inc. has sought ways to require developers to pay the costs of bringing *colonia* water systems up to health department standards. Using the Deceptive Trade Practices Act, they have had some success in getting developers to work with water supply corporations. These corporations have also been asked to reduce meter installation fees and eliminate waiting periods to obtain meters. In most instances, *colonia* residents have worked with water supply corporations to help resolve problems, raise money, and provide labor to construct water systems.[27]

Regional groups have worked to alleviate many of the problems existing in the *colonias*. The Lower Rio Grande Development Council (LRGDC) is one of 24 councils of government in the state. It was formed in 1967 as a sub-state planning region to address regional issues and development needs. The council has implemented several major projects dealing with water and waste water planning and management for *colonias*. It has identified significant water quality problems, formulated alternatives, recommended cost effective solutions, and provided current monitoring of conditions. Along with the Texas Water Development Board, the LRGDC collected and evaluated data on more than a thousand rural and suburban communities to help design a regional system to reduce the problems faced by the rural population.[28]

A second regional group interested in the problems of the LRGV is Valley Interfaith, a coalition of 36 churches representing more than 50,000 families in Cameron, Hidalgo, Starr, and Willacy counties. This group works to give the poor and politically disenfranchised citizens vehicles for participation in the democratic process. Working with a sister organization, El Paso Interreligious Sponsoring Organization (EPISO), Valley Interfaith has proposed a "New Deal for the Border." This initiative, which would be sponsored by the federal government, would:[29]

· Establish a $500 million pool for the development of water and sewers in the *colonias*. This money would supplement current and future city and state funds and bring down the cost to the people of building sewer and water facilities.
· Provide a series of grants and low-interest loans to families for connection to sewer systems. These would help residents bring indoor plumbing already in place up to city standards.
· Increase the appropriation of Community Development Block Grant funds for cities and other government entities affected by *colonias*. These funds could provide infrastructure such as roads, drainage, and parks.
· Develop alternative affordable housing options. Rural areas have become attractive because proper housing in cities has been lacking.
· Develop a comprehensive job training and public works program that addresses both infrastructure needs and job needs.
· Maintain a high level of educational funding for public educational institutions along the border.
· Maintain grants and scholarships for minority students.

Individual counties have also attempted to address the *colonia* problem, though they have very little statutory authority. Subdivision plots in Cameron county must receive Commissioners Court approval before developers can sell lots. Efforts are underway to require developers to adhere to the requirements for new subdivisions set forth in the 1989 state legislation. In addition, the FmHA funded water projects more of than $9 million between 1978 and 1988. Some of these funds have been used by nonprofit water supply corporations to extend potable water to *colonias.*[30]

Subdivision regulations in Hidalgo county also require Commissioners Court approval before lots can be sold. Since March, 1987, new rural subdivisions have been required to have potable water and adequate sewage disposal facilities. In an attempt to monitor growth, the county now requires building permits for all rural construction projects. For those *colonia* already in existence, Community Development Block Grants have funded water lines to some *colonia* residents. Additional water improvement projects to about 90% of Hidalgo *colonias* have been funded by four nonprofit water supply corporations servicing the county. FmHA loans and grants helped support these projects.[31]

Since June, 1988, Starr County has required that proposed rural subdivision plats guarantee that residents have access to both potable water and some sort of approved sewage system. If a public sewer system is not available, approved septic tanks or sewage treatment plants must be provided. For those *colonias* already in existence, FmHA funds have been used to extend water lines to some *colonias* and to fund a water treatment facility.[32]

Willacy county had done little to combat the *colonia* problem. Subdivisions are regulated by ordinances and state health regulations only to the extent needed to comply with the National Flood Insurance Program. Potable water and waste water facilities are not required in rural subdivisions. Little has been done to apply for water/sewer assistance.[33]

A number of measures requiring federal assistance that would increase the economic ability of *colonia* residents to afford better living conditions, raise the level of health awareness, and provide appropriate utility services have been proposed by counties containing *colonias.* These measures include:[34]

- Funding earmarked specifically for residents of *colonias* to be used for adult education in English language fluency, health education, and job training.
- Grants or low-interest loans for domestic utility hook-ups, funding to be earmarked specifically for residents whose income level is below minimum income levels designated for currently existing programs.
- Help in finding new construction funds administered through existing housing assistance programs with income level requirements below current FHA limitations.
- Continued federal support of all funding programs geared towards

building and expanding public, private, and mutual domestic sewer
and water systems.
· Federal investigation into and support of methods of addressing illegal subdivisions.

The efforts made at all levels have been encouraging. However, a number
of obstacles remain that prevent solutions. The budget problems that exist
at the federal, state, and local levels cast a pall over even the most simple
plans.

3.5 Conclusion

Understanding the nature of the people that live in *colonias* and the
socio-economic environment in which they exist is an important part of
dealing with *colonias* and their role in the life of the LRGV. Despite their
grimness, *colonias* provide homes to thousands of people. They are an
"inevitable transition of the border region from a rural zone into a
complex, urban, and primarily Mexican-American community."[35]
    To begin solving the problems in the *colonias*, the communication gap
must be bridged. A massive education campaign should be undertaken
involving not only educational institutions, but public agencies as well.
Proper education could eliminate many of the problems which occur
simply as a result of misinformation and the inability to understand the
available options.
    A second campaign should focus on health problems. A healthier
environment will have beneficial effects for all the Valley. Productivity
will increase if workers and students have fewer sick days. Less money
will be needed for health care and services. This benefits both the
agencies which provide health care and the family budgets of those who
must pay for health care. Finally, the communicable diseases that exist in
the *colonias* have the potential to spread throughout the LRGV and the
southern part of the state of Texas.
    It is clear, then, that in the short run, local governments and/or residents
need immediate financial assistance. In the long run, an economic
development plan is needed much like the one adopted for Appalachia in
the 1960s and 1970s. Such a plan should work to create jobs, encourage
private investment in the region, develop an infrastructure, promote
entrepreneurship, and alleviate such problems as illiteracy, infant
mortality, and inadequate health care.

Notes

1. *Colonias in the Lower Rio Grande Valley of South Texas: Policy Research Project Report No. 18* (Austin, TX: LBJ School of Public Affairs, 1977), p. 5.

2. Testimony by Exiquio Salinas, Director of Management Studies, Texas Department of Human Services before the U.S. House of Representatives Select Committee on Hunger, May 15, 1989.

3. *Colonias in the Lower Rio Grande Valley of South Texas*, p. 9.

4. Office of Strategic Management, Research, and Development, *The Colonias Factbook: A Survey of Living Conditions in Rural Areas of South Texas and West Texas Border Counties* (Austin, TX: Texas Department of Human Services, 1988), p. 6-3.

5. *Ibid.*, p. iii.

6. F. Gibney, Jr., "In Texas, a Grim New Appalachia," *Newsweek* (June 8, 1987): p.27-28.

7. *Colonias in the Lower Rio Grande Valley*, p. 5.

8. See *Ibid.*, pp. 14-15 for a complete description of land-use policies.

9. See Resources, Community, and Economic Development Division, *Rural Development: Problems and Progress of Colonia Subdivisions Near Mexico Border* (Washington, DC: U.S. General Accounting Office, 1990) for descriptions of the four counties of the LRGV.

10. Testimony by Hon. Mickey Leland before the U.S. House of Representatives Select Committee on Hunger, May 15, 1989.

11. Testimony by Evonne Charboneau, Attorney, Texas Rural Legal Aid, Inc. before the U.S. House of Representatives Select Committee on Hunger, May 15, 1989.

12. See *The Colonia Factbook*.

13. *Colonias in the Lower Rio Grande Valley*, p. 11.

14. *Ibid.*, p. 12.

15. *Ibid.*

16. *Ibid.*, p. 11.

17. Testimony by H. Applegate, Research Associate at the Center for Inter-American and Border Studies in El Paso before the U.S. House of Representatives Select Committee on Public Works and Transportation, March 12, 1988.

18. See *The Colonia Factbook*.

19. Testimony by Exiquio Salinas.

20. Testimony by Hon. Mickey Leland.

21. Gibney, p. 28.

22. Testimony by the Texas Water Development Board to the U.S. House of Representatives Select Committee on Public Works and Transportation, March 12, 1988.

23. *Ibid.*

24. *Rural Development*, p. 11.

25. *Ibid.*

26. See Texas Senate Committee on Natural Resources, *Interim Report to the 70th Legislature*, January, 1987.

27. Testimony by Evonne Carboneau.

28. Testimony by K. Jones, Assistant Executive Director, Lower Rio Grande Valley Development Council to U.S. House of Representatives Select Committee on Public Works and Transportation, March 12, 1988.

29. Testimony by M. Martinez, representative of EPISO to U.S. House of Representatives Select Committee on Public Works and Transportation, March 12, 1988.

30. *Rural Development*, p. 19.

31. *Ibid.*, pp. 16-17.

32. *Ibid.*, p. 22.

33. *Ibid.*, p. 20.

34. Testimony by S. Allen to U.S. House of Representatives Select Committee on Public Works and Transportation, March 12, 1988.

35. Testimony by A. Boyd. Superintendent of the San Elizario Independent School District to U.S. House of Representatives Public Works Sub-Committee on Water Resources, March 11, 1988.

4

The Maquiladora Industry
and Economic Development

4.1 Introduction

The maquiladora industry plays an important role in the Mexican economy. As a contributor to Mexico's foreign exchange, it ranks second behind oil exports ($10.1 billion in 1990) and ahead of tourism, Mexico's third largest source of foreign exchange ($1.5 billion).[1] Of the $3.84 billion generated by maquiladoras in 1990, more than one-third (38%) went to workers employed in the plants (see Table 4.1). Much of the rest of the income generated by maquiladoras entered the economy through rents, taxes, payments for materials, national production of raw materials, and other miscellaneous costs.

Its relative economic importance has prompted much national and international attention from the media, labor groups, politicians, business-men, and scholars. The "pessimists" among this group include both Mexicans and Americans. Nationalistic Mexican political leaders and leftist scholars bemoan what they perceive to be the loss of internal control over Mexico's economic future. Feminists argue that the predomi-nantly female workers in the maquiladoras are exploited. Union leaders worry because most of the maquiladora workers are not unionized and show little sign of becoming so. And many of the long-time residents of the historic border cities find the rapid and uncontrolled growth of the area unattractive.[2]

On the American side of the border, many workers in border areas feel the maquiladoras have cost them their jobs. They are joined in their "pessimistic" view by much of the border patrol and INS officials who attribute the increase in illegal border crossings to the lure of border factories. Left-wing American scholars disapprove of the low wages and the capital investment that connotes "Yankee imperialism."[3]

TABLE 4.1

Overview of the Maquiladora Industry, October 1990

	LRGV	MRGV	URGV	Total Texas Borderland	Total U.S. Borderland
Plants	187	282	382	857	2014
% of total	21.8[a]	34.0[a]	33.6[a]	42.6[b]	
Workers	64,287	66,241	171,468	301,9964	68,392
% of total	21.3[a]	21.9[a]	56.8[a]	64.5[b]	
Value Added ($mil)	481.8	376.7	999.1	1857.6	2862.6
% of total	25.9[a]	20.3[a]	53.8[a]	64.9[b]	
Imp. Raw Mat.($mil)	1950.6	913.2	2702.8	5566.3	8618.2
% of total	35.0[a]	16.4[a]	48.6[a]	64.6[b]	
Wages, Salaries, and Benefits ($mil)	244.0	161.8	558.7	964.6	1449.0
% of total	25.3[a]	16.8[a]	57.9[a]	66.6[b]	

Notes: LRGV includes the state Tamaulipas (except the City of Nuevo Laredo)
MRGV includes the state of Nuevo Leon, Coahuila, and Nuevo Laredo City
URGV includes the state of Chihuahua
a: percentage of total for Texas borderland
b: percentage of total for U.S. borderland

Source: National Institute of Statistics, Geography and Informatics. *Statistics of the Maquiladora Industry of Exportation.* Mexico City: INEGI, 1991.

There are many, however, on both sides of the border who feel that the maquiladora industry yields many benefits. Among these "optimists" are the Mexican *políticos* who collect fees for public services. In addition, they believe that the border factories help relieve unemployment and reduce some of the strains on local social services. Mexican investors benefit from leases of industrial parks to foreign companies who set up the border factories, while private transportation companies enjoy increased business from moving both inputs and outputs to and from the border.[4]

American merchants appreciate the increased retail trade as workers spend a portion of their wages in the U.S. on food, clothing, and recreation. Those firms in the U.S. which supply inputs to the maquiladora industry also benefit from any success experienced by the border industries. Further, the application of Mexican labor to American component parts allows U.S. corporations to compete more effectively in global markets.[5]

In many ways, both the "pessimists" and the "optimists" make valid points. The issues are complex and continue to change. It is apparent, however, that the maquiladora industry significantly affects the social and economic development of the LRGV.

4.2 Historic Development of the Border Economy

The term *maquiladora* is of Arabic origin (*makila*) and comes from the Spanish verb *maquilar*, meaning "to mill for a fee." Mexican farmers once took their grain to a mill to be ground into flour. As payment to the mill owner for the grinding, they would leave a portion of the grain known as the *maquila*.[6] Today, *maquila* refers to the process of production and assembly operations utilizing large numbers of unskilled workers, while *maquiladora* refers to assembly or manufacturing operations or factories.[7] The maquiladoras of Mexico combine inexpensive Mexican labor with materials, technology, and capital from other countries to produce goods primarily for export.

Modern Mexican border industrialization began in 1933. To protect local retail markets from the vagaries of a world-wide depression while attempting to maintain a higher standard of living for the rapidly growing border population, the Mexican government created limited free zone areas along the Mexico-U.S. border. As the border population became an increasingly important part of the national economy, a dual policy system emerged. Strategies were developed to increase industrialization and to further economic development so that families moving from the interior to the border could be accommodated. Numerous programs were put forward which increased the trade and interdependency between Mexico and the United States.[8]

One such program was initiated in 1961. The National Border Program (Programa Nacional Fronterizo or PRONAF) provided physical improvements such as roads, industrial parks, railway lines, electricity, water, and factory buildings. The goal was to promote commercial and industrial development and tourism.[9] For several years, regional products were produced and sold, primarily to tourists. Despite these efforts, the original plan failed to provide the economic impetus desired. The problem was made more acute in 1964 when the U.S. House of Representatives dissolved the Bracero Program (P.L. 78) which had allowed large-scale importation of Mexican agricultural labor into the United States.

To cope with the increased level of unemployment the failure of both PRONAF and the Bracero Program had created in northern Mexico, the

Mexican government began to "informally" permit foreign investments in the northern border states. They also instituted a program to encourage retail sales. Mexican merchants were allowed to import U.S.- made goods (*artículos ganchos*) duty-free and sell them at prices equal to or lower than those charged by American shops. These policies also failed to adequately stimulate Mexican production and employment. Manufacturing employment absorbed very little of the workforce in Mexican border municipalities. Most of the employment remained in agriculture, mining, and service activities and many continued to seek work in U.S. border cities.[10]

During this period, a second, more formal program called the Border Industrialization Program (BIP) was announced and became effective in 1966. This plan was designed to once again encourage industrial development along the 2000-mile border Mexico shares with the United States. It provided American businesses with a number of advantages:[11]

(1) 100% ownership and control by foreigners of companies operating in Mexico;
(2) permits for duty-free imports of raw materials, component parts, machinery, and production equipment, provided all such items were re-exported;
(3) special immigration permits for foreign managers, technicians, and supervisors;
(4) the setting up of a 30-year trust to allow foreigners to own land and buildings in the restricted coastal and border areas.

Throughout the late 1960s and the 1970s, the maquiladora industry (as the BIP came to be known) grew from a low of 57 plants in 1966 to a total of more than 2000 in 1990. Between 1986 and 1990, maquiladora plants increased at an average rate of 21.2% while employment increased at an average rate of 15.6% per year. Such growth yielded an average of 257 new plants and 49,106 new jobs in each of the five years of this period. In 1990, goods produced in maquiladora plants represented 37% of Mexico's total manufactured exports and maquiladora employment, located primarily along the border, represented 2% of Mexico's total formal employment.[12]

Maquiladoras are also called "in-bond" plants. Prior to assembling the imported inputs, each plant must give a "guarantee" that it will pay import taxes on machinery, equipment, and primary materials or components as required by Mexican tax laws. These guarantees can take several forms: pledge of assets, a bond issued by an authorized bonding company, a cash deposit, or a deposit in a bonded warehouse. Apart from this guarantee, maquiladoras pay no other import taxes on machinery and materials. In this way, these plants are "in-bond" until they export their finished product. In recent years, the requirements for "in-bond" status have been relaxed to encourage continued growth of the industry.

The maquiladora industry has also played an important role in the overall U.S. economy, providing labor-intensive activities to complement American capital-intensive manufacturing. In 1987, U.S. imports from Mexico had the highest duty-free content of any other imports, comprising 35% of the worldwide import total. During this same year, 52% of all maquiladora imports were made up of U.S. components, while imports from other countries counted U.S. components as only 19% of the total. The higher U.S. content in Mexican imports implies that Mexican maquiladoras are much more integrated in the American economy.[13]

Many of the border factories are known as "twin plants" because a second plant exists on the U.S. side of the border for finishing the products which are imported to the U.S. Often, however, the U.S. plant is not located in a border "sister city". It has been estimated that some maquiladoras obtain less than one-fifth of their materials and components from an adjacent U.S. border city.[14] Instead, interior cities such as Fort Wayne, Indiana; Aurora and Chicago, Illinois; and Portland, Oregon have plants with direct links to maquiladoras. Most so-called "twin plants" are already established plants which serve as suppliers to their Mexican counterpart. Thus, the twin plant concept impacts a region far beyond the Mexico-U.S. border. Plants, materials, and employees are located and come from all over the United States.

4.3 Twin Plants in Mexico's LRGV

The maquiladora industry in the LRGV encompasses the border *municipios* of Matamoras, Reynosa, and Camargo-Rio Bravo in the state of Tamaulipas in the northeastern part of Mexico. Table 4.1 compares the number of plants and workers in the maquiladora industry in the Lower, Middle, and Upper Rio Grande Valley with the state of Texas and the U.S. as a whole for 1990. While the plants of the LRGV account for less than 22% of the Texas total and only about 13% of Mexico's total, they nevertheless play an important role in understanding the subject matter of this study.

Matamoros

The number of maquiladora plants in Matamoros totaled 93 in October, 1990 (see Table 4.2). This reflected an increase of 8.1% from the previous

TABLE 4.2

Border *Municipios* Maquiladoras, January - October 1990

Indicator	Matamoros[a]	Reynosa[b]	RioBravo[c]
No. Of Plants (monthly average)	93	59	35
No. of Workers	38,305	22,918	3,064
Direct Labor	31,737	17,207	2,475
Men	9,977	6,279	756
Women	21,760	10,928	1,719
Technicians	4,172	2,623	333
Administrative	2,396	3,088	256
Gross Production ($mil)	1610.8	753.5	68.0
Mexican Value Added ($mil)	311.7	151.6	18.5
Imp. Raw Materials ($mil)	1299.1	602.0	49.5
Mex. Raw Materials (4mil)	10.8	10.9	2.7
Wages, Salaries, Benefits ($mil)	156.4	81.3	6.4
Ave. Wage, incl. benefits ($/hr)	1.91	1.72	1.72

a: across from Brownsville, TX
b: across from McAllen, TX
c: across from Rio Grande City, TX

Source: Calculations based on data from the National Institute of Statistics, Geography and Informatics. *Statistics of the Maquiladora Industry of Exportation.* Mexico City: INEGI, 1991.

year. The industry's total employment reached 38,305, an increase of 1.4%. Direct labor (*obreros*) represented 82.9% of the total number of workers, 68.6% of which were females. Of the total employees, 10.9% were technicians while another 6.2% were administrative workers.

This same year, the maquiladora industry's output totaled $1.6 billion. While this may sound impressive, Mexican value-added comprised less than 20% of the total. The value of raw materials processed totaled an equally impressive $1.3 billion though the Mexican share of raw materials made up merely 0.8% of the total. Wages and salaries, including benefits, totaled $156.4 million in 1990, up 31.1% from the $119.3 million of 1989.

As in most industrial twin cities, the maquiladora industry in Matamoros relies heavily on the services available from its U.S. counterpart. Equipment, tools, and machinery are purchased throughout the U.S. and serviced in Brownsville. Most companies in Matamoros use financial services and rent warehousing space in Brownsville. All transportation used by the twin plants goes out of Brownsville. This includes truck, rail, and UPS. It has been estimated that Mexican maquiladora workers spent $8.8 million (an average of 5.6% of their income) in the area.[15]. Adding this to the value of imported raw materials means that Matamoros' maquiladora industry sent $1.3 billion through the U.S. economy between January and October of 1990. Clearly, the maquiladora industry has provided strong economic support to the Brownsville economy.

Reynosa

Reynosa was home to 59 maquiladora plants in October, 1990, an increase of 1.7% from the previous year (see Table 4.2). The industry's total employment decreased 3.3% to 22,918 of which 63.5% were female. Technicians represented 11.4% and administrative workers 13.5% of the total number employed.

During the period, the maquiladora industry in Reynosa had a production value of $753.5 million. Mexican value added was $151.6 million with imported raw materials accounting for $602 million. Only 1.8% of the raw materials processed were of Mexican origin. Wages, salaries, and benefits equaled $81.3 million with an average wage level the same as that of Matamoros.

The maquiladora industry in Reynosa has a significant impact on its "sister city", McAllen. Between January and October of 1990, Mexican workers spent $4.6 million in McAllen (an average of 5.6% of their income). If the value of the materials imported to Reynosa is included, the total rises to $606.6 million. This total excludes money generated by direct expenditures and services in the McAllen area by the industry. It also fails to account for income created by such jobs as additional service sector workers and transportation workers. Thus, jobs directly connected to the maquiladora industry and indirectly related to it through multiplier effects have been created on both sides of the border.

Camargo-Rio Bravo

Prior to 1980, no maquiladora plants operated in the Camargo-Rio Bravo area. By October, 1990, 35 plants employing more than 3000 workers were in operation (see Table 4.2). Like Matamoros and Reynosa, the majority of the employees were female (69.5%). Technicians comprised 10.9% of the workers and 8.3% were administrative personnel.

Output for the Camargo-Rio Bravo maquiladora industry totaled $68 million including $18.5 million in Mexican value-added. The Mexican share of the raw materials processed was 5.1%, or $2.7 million of a total of $52.2 million. Wages (averaging $1.63 per hour), salaries, and benefits for the period totaled $6.4 million.

Between the value of imported material and the portion of the incomes of Mexican workers spent in Rio Grande City, the maquiladora industry in Camargo-Rio Bravo sent $49.9 million through the U.S. economy between January and October of 1990. Once again, this figure excludes multiplier effects on employment, income spent on transportation, taxes, and lease payments for warehousing space on the U.S. side of the border.

The economic impact of the maquiladora plants located in the Mexican border *municipios* of Matamoros, Reynosa, and Camargo-Rio Bravo in the LRGV area has been significant. The first ten months of 1990 saw the generation of almost $1.4 billion in income for the U.S. as plants purchased raw materials and Mexican maquiladora workers spent an average of 5.6% of their income on U.S. goods and services.[16] This has translated into increased employment, particularly in the border area. In addition to the trade and service sector jobs that complement maquiladora activity, employment in the manufacturing sector has been affected as well. For every 1½ jobs created in the trade sector, an additional job has been created in the manufacturing sector (see Section 4.8 below).[17] As mentioned in Chapter 1, it is important to remember that the economic links between these "sister cities" existed long before the coming of the BIP and the maquiladoras. Economic conditions on one side have typically affected the other.

4.4 Labor in the Maquiladora Industry

One of the objectives of the BIP was to increase employment in the border region. The maquiladoras helped to meet that objective, employing more than 64,000 workers in the LRGV alone. This figure does not include support enterprises which would add thousands more to the total. The attention given the maquila labor force in recent years has focused on low wage rates, high turnover rates, reliance on female employment, and impact on illegal immigration. All of these issues have some bearing on the level of poverty in the region.

Much of the strength of the BIP rests on the relative low wages available in Mexico. These low wages enable other countries, particularly the United States, to import raw materials to the border region for assembly and re-export. Such a policy enables high wage countries to be more competitive in world markets. Despite their low level, the wages paid in the maquiladora plants are among the highest in Mexico. Without these "high" wages, poverty in the state of Tamaulipas would be even greater than it currently is.

Wages in Mexico are not determined by the usual supply and demand of factor markets. Instead, the government designates local minimum wages based upon the cost-of-living for each of 111 specific areas in the country.[18] These minimum wages vary, however, with the category of worker. The three basic categories of wages for the maquiladora factories include:[19]

(1) assembly-line or production workers (*obreros*)
(2) "professional" positions such as technicians, maintenance personnel, repairmen, etc.
(3) administrative positions, secretarial and clerical staff, nurses, etc.

Wages have risen over time in the industry. In 1990, the average hourly wage for *obrero* labor rose $1.91 in Matamoros, a 21.6% increase from the previous year. Technicians saw a 10.9% increase to $4.78 per hour, while administrators earned $5.23 per hour, a 10.5% increase. Since wages are linked to the cost of living, upward trends in wages depend, at least in part, on the rate of inflation. The government has been following a tight exchange rate policy in recent years in an attempt to control run-away inflation and has enjoyed some success. Table 4.3 lists wage rates for twelve of the production sectors. Machinery, tools, and medical instruments top the list, while the lowest wages are paid to workers in the textile and apparel sector.

The wage levels set by the government do not include worker benefits. American-owned maquiladoras typically allow for as much as 110% of the minimum wage and make a number of benefits available for workers. Bonuses are given for promptness and attendance and for production increases. Transportation services, cafeteria facilities, and education are subsidized. The plants also offer medical and savings plans. In addition to these more formal benefits, many plants sponsor athletic teams and beauty pageants, send flowers to celebrate birthdays, and provide other

TABLE 4.3

Composition by Sector: Matamoros, Reynosa, Rio Bravo, 1990

Production Sector	Plants(%)	Employment(%)	For. Inputs(%)	Wages($/hr)
1. Electric/Electronics	27.6	51.5	99.2	1.61
2. Machinery and Tools	16.0	9.8	98.3	2.24
3. Transportation Equip.	10.9	22.7	98.4	1.83
4. Chemicals, etc.	13.5	3.6	99.0	1.53
5. Textiles and Apparel	8.3	1.8	98.1	1.28
6. Footwear/Leather Goods	5.1	1.7	83.2	1.42
7. Food	4.2	1.9	64.5	1.44
8. Manf. Goods: Glass	1.9	0.5	62.2	1.53
9. Manf. Goods: Paper	1.4	0.7	79.3	1.54
10.Medical Instruments	1.4	1.0	99.3	2.24
11.Furniture and Wood/Metal	1.4	0.6	95.7	1.54
12.Toys and Sporting Goods	0.7	2.8	98.2	1.97
	100.0	100.0		

Source: Statistics of the Maquilidora Industry of Exportation. Mexico City: INEGI, 1991.

services. All such perks add to the quality of life for the employees.[20] Benefits of this nature are less likely to be available in maquiladoras owned by Mexicans.

The ability of employer-provided benefits to improve the quality of life for workers is tempered somewhat by turnover rates of more than 100%. Many assembly-line and production employees, mainly females, move from factory to factory seeking better working conditions and/or benefits. Others leave temporarily because of the death of a parent or the health problems of a family member who requires care. Some females leave work when they marry and start their families, while others leave to continue their education. Federally-mandated exit interviews show that very few workers quit because of poor working conditions, though many object to the government-controlled minimum wage.[21] For the most part, workers, particularly those at the lower levels living in *colonias,* appear to benefit from the informal social networks provided by the maquiladoras.

Almost 67% of the *obrero* workers employed in the LRGV border maquiladoras are female (see Table 4.2). Occupational segregation has existed throughout the history of border development and is not a product of the maquiladoras. This contemporary pattern is merely an extension of an accepted practice and not a deliberate attempt by U.S. employers to exploit females. Wage levels for specific jobs are the same for both men and women, though men appear to have greater access to the better paying technical jobs. Most plant managers and administrators find the greater dexterity of females makes them more suitable for assembly-line work. Dexterity tests given as part of the hiring process support this conclusion. As the level of technical expertise has risen in U.S. owned maquiladoras, increased hiring of males has taken place. The percentage of male workers in the industry has increased from less than 5% in the early days of the BIP to 35% in recent years.[22] If this trend persists, some of the unemployment of males that currently exists in the LRGV could be alleviated.[23] This would also provide an attractive alternative to males who might otherwise immigrate illegally to the U.S.

A young, predominantly female labor force does not usually lend itself to unionization. This is not true for the maquiladora workers in Tamaulipas, however. The maquiladora industry as a whole has opposed the organization of plants by unions and has worked to prevent such organization with some support from the Mexican government. In Tamaulipas, the unions hold some power and have managed to unionize nearly all of the factories. The industry cooperates and tries to accommodate labor's needs by providing adequate fringe benefits such as those mentioned above. Communication between management and workers is nurtured as well.[24] Efforts in this regard help mitigate the less attractive qualities of life on the border.

Maquiladoras also provide training opportunities which allow workers to upgrade their skills. Mexican law requires companies operating as maquiladoras to train at least 25% of their workforce either for their current position or for promotion. Many of the larger companies provide formal classroom training as well as on-the-job training. Such training allows some workers to advance from line operations, to trainer, to supervisor, and finally to inspector. Despite a lack of education beyond primary school, managers report that Mexican labor is not only trainable and reliable, but is often as productive as U.S. labor. As computers enter the maquila process, productivity should continue to climb.[25]

The increasing need for technical expertise in the maquiladoras has encouraged many young Mexicans to attend local technological institutes and universities. Careers in the maquiladoras appear as attractive options to employment in other sectors of the Mexican economy. The educational sector has responded in recent years by adding programs to meet industry needs. In general, the economic gains achieved by these maquiladora workers mirror those of the U.S. rather than those of Mexican workers in the interior.[26]

4.5 The Structure of the Maquiladora Industry

The maquiladora industry in the LRGV is comprised of twelve main sectors producing a wide range of products. Table 4.3 lists the sectors along with employment and input information for each sector. The figures include only those maquiladora plants in Matamoros, Reynosa, and Rio Bravo.

Electric and Electronics dominates the maquiladora industry, producing primarily television receivers and other consumer electronic products; electronic components such as semiconductors, television picture tubes, connectors, relays, and switches; office machines and computers; and telephone and telegraph apparatus. In 1990, the number of plants in this rapidly growing sector represented 27.6% of the total maquiladora plants in the region and employed 51.5% of the entire industry labor force. This sector imported nearly all (99.2%) of its inputs and tends to be highly integrated into the production and marketing networks of its affiliated U.S. firms.

Transportation Equipment consists primarily of automotive parts and accessories. It is the second largest sector of the LRGV maquiladora industry. Trade in this sector has also experienced rapid growth in recent years. In 1990, this sector employed 22.7% of the industry labor force and comprised 10.9% of the total plants. This sector also imported nearly all of its inputs (98.4%).

Machinery and Tools is a sector that complements the U.S. production of these products and includes primarily machine tools and household appliances such as washing machines, refrigerators, and gas ranges. In 1990, this sector employed 9.8% of the total maquila labor force in the region and made up 16% of the total plants. Once again, most of its inputs (98.3%) were imported.

Chemical and Related Products includes petrochemicals and pharmaceuticals. This sector has accelerated its output of major chemicals in recent years and accounted for 13.5% of the plants in the region in 1990. Employment in this sector utilized 3.6% of the regional maquila labor force. Nearly 100% of its inputs came from foreign sources.

Textiles and Apparel produces clothing of all types. It has also experienced rapid growth, particularly in the garment industry. The technology in this sector is not very modern but employed 1.8% of the industry labor force. Maquiladoras in this sector comprised 8.3% of the total in the region and imported 98.1% of their inputs.

Footwear and Leather Goods includes factories engaged in tanning, currying, and finishing hides and skins as well as those which manufacture finished leather and artificial leather products. This sector imported just 83.2% of its inputs and used less than 2% of the regional industry labor force in 1990. Plants in this sector accounted for 5.1% of the regional total.

Food includes factories which manufacture or process foods and beverages for human consumption, and certain related products such as chewing gum, vegetable and animal fats and oils, and prepared feeds for animals and fowls. In 1990, the food sector represented 4.2% of the regional total and employed 1.9% of the regional industry labor force. Almost 65% of the inputs in this sector were imported.

Glassware includes fiberglass, glass containers, household glassware, and miscellaneous glass products such as laboratory glassware and glass blocks. The plants in this sector made up 1.9% of the regional total and employed 0.5% of the regional industry workforce. The glassware sector imported just over 62% of its inputs in 1990.

Paper Products is another manufactured goods sector which produces paperboard from wood pulp and other fibers. It also manufactures converted paperboard products. It comprised 1.4% of the regional total. Less than 1% of the regional industry workforce were employed in this sector. Foreign inputs made up over 79% of this sector's inputs.

Medical Instruments manufactures medical, surgical, ophthalmic, and veterinary instruments and apparatus. It employed 1% of the total regional maquila labor force and comprised 1.4% of the total plants. Foreign inputs processed by this sector accounted for almost all (99.3%) of the total in 1990.

Furniture and Wood/Metal Fixtures includes household, office, public building, and restaurant furniture, as well as office and store fixtures. It comprised 1.4% of the total regional plants and employed 0.7% of the labor force. In 1990, nearly 96% of this sectors inputs were imported.

Toys and Sporting Goods made up the smallest number of the regional maquiladora plants (0.7%) in 1990. However, it employed 2.8% of the regional labor force and imported 98.2% of its inputs. This sector produces games and game sets for adults and children, mechanical and nonmechanical toys, sporting and athletic goods, and gymnasium and playground equipment.

The maquiladora industry in the LRGV produces a wide range of products with predominantly semi-skilled labor. As is evident from the descriptions given above, most of the inputs are imported thereby stimulating very little internal trade with Mexico. The LRGV benefits primarily from the jobs created, both in the factories themselves and in the related service industries, and the wages received which help alleviate poverty in the area and fuel the local economy.

4.6 The "New" Maquiladoras

The original BIP called for the development of plants along a 2-kilometer section of the border between Mexico and the United States. In 1983, President De La Madrid revised the laws, making it easier to set up and operate a maquiladora. The new Mexican Industrial Program (MIP) allowed maquiladoras to sell some of their output in Mexico and encouraged them to locate in the interior of the country, particularly in the less developed regions. De La Madrid's successor, President Salinas, issued an additional decree in December, 1989 which simplified the acquisition of maquiladora permits even further and extended duty-free status to subcontractors and service companies supplying maquiladoras. Interior maquiladoras were once again encouraged in order to better integrate the industry with domestic suppliers.[27]   Consequently, the growth of maquiladoras in the interior has grown dramatically, though more than three-fourths can still be found in the border area.[28]

These changes in Mexico's regional development program were accompanied by a change in the overall nature of the maquiladora industry. Worker productivity has increased as the industry has become more capital intensive. Value added per worker in constant pesos was an average of 189 million between 1975 and 1981. Between 1982 and 1990, this average rose to 217 million pesos. Skilled workers for the early period averaged 9% of the workforce and rose to an average of 13% for the later period. With increasing capital intensity in the form of sophisticated computer operations and robotics, labor costs as a proportion of total costs have declined. The average for the 1975-1981 period was 18% while labor costs in the 1982-1990 period fell to just 12% of total operating costs.[29]   An acceleration of this trend could have mixed effects for the industry. On the positive side, productivity increases could lead to higher wages, though this has yet to happen. It could also increase the attractiveness of maquiladoras if institutional constraints such as union rules, etc. prevent the adoption of robotics or other capital-intensive innovations. On the negative side, as the industry becomes more capital intensive, foreign firms seeking to lower total costs by using large quantities of cheap labor will have fewer incentives to move production to Mexico. It was Mexico's elastic supply of cheap labor that played a prominent role in the original growth of the industry.

Since 1982, the number of maquiladoras has increased by more than 230%. The number of plants located in the interior of Mexico has increased by more than 350%.[30]   This growth in the number of interior maquiladoras could decrease immigration from the interior to the LRGV with potential positive effects on poverty and unemployment. However, any decrease in the number of jobs in the border maquiladoras would offset these gains. The Texas counties in the LRGV are also affected by the growth in interior maquiladoras. Unlike their border counterparts, interior maquiladoras tend to rely more on domestic suppliers, thereby decreasing their dependence on American or Texas suppliers. They also typically use fewer American services and technical personnel. Their workers have fewer opportunities to spend their incomes in Texas border cities, though the Valley is still a popular vacation spot for many Mexicans. The Mexican government is actively offering incentives to

Mexican firms willing to become suppliers to interior maquiladoras. As the border becomes more crowded, the tendency for maquiladoras to locate in the interior will increase. Any plan for the economic development of the LRGV must take this into account. At present, the majority of those maquiladoras currently located on the border have no plans to relocate (see Chapter 6).

4.7 Flexible Manufacturing and the Maquiladora Industry

The maquiladora industry arose at a time when mass production, marked by vertical integration and large inventories, dominated the industrial sector. The international division of labor appeared to be a rational way to decrease costs and remain competitive in an increasingly competitive world. In recent years, however, a more flexible strategy has come to dominate corporate strategies seeking lower costs and higher productivity as they face increasing global competitiveness. Flexible production calls for just-in-time inventories and close links with important suppliers. This not only affects costs and productivity, but encourages fewer but larger, long-term suppliers as well.[31]

The effect of this new corporate strategy on the role of maquiladoras has prompted two opposing arguments. One theory holds that as American firms adopt flexible production to keep up with the Japanese, Mexico (and the border region) will lose jobs and revenues. With a shortened product cycle, product development and production will tend to locate near one another thereby eliminating the spatial division of labor that characterizes the maquiladora industry.

This shortened product cycle would also allow for rapid innovation which would, in turn, decrease the pressure for reducing labor costs. Labor cost would also become less of a factor with the flexible automation that this particular corporate strategy utilizes. Production could then return to the higher wage regions of the home country. These higher wage regions are more likely to have the multi-skilled and experienced labor force required by the technology associated with flexible production.[32]

A shortened product cycle also requires suppliers to share technology, technical assistance, quality surveillance, and specialized capital equipment repair services. Joint ventures between producers and suppliers become more attractive with the increasing integration. Offshore locations could pose problems for firms engaging in flexible production if limited technical skills or transportation facilities existed.[33]

A counterargument suggests that an offshore, cheap labor location and flexible production are not necessarily incompatible. In a world dominated by sophisticated telecommunications, computers, and rapid air travel, distances become inconsequential. Mexico is only hours away by air from all parts of the United States and just minutes away from the LRGV. Furthermore, given the concentration of existing maquiladoras along the Mexico-Texas border, suppliers could easily relocate to take advantage of this concentration. A few strategically-placed suppliers in the LRGV, for example, could service the entire state of Tamaulipas as well as neighboring Nuevo Leon and Coahuila.[34]

Labor also plays a role in the counterarguments. Just as competition makes cheap labor attractive to conventional mass production, flexible producers could also benefit from lower labor costs as well. As automation becomes more sophisticated, "button-pushers" and "set-up technicians" could replace the more skilled workers flexible production currently requires. A relatively inexpensive and less skilled workforce such as that found on both sides of the Rio Grande could then be a cost-effective asset.[35]

Lastly, surveys indicate that flexible production such as that which is currently employed in the U.S. and Japan will not be adopted all at once. Automated production processes have been introduced in Mexico. However, as of 1990, no plants were fully automated. In addition, the United States has continued to supply those plants which have adopted flexible production, leaving intact the original "twin plant" relationship. It would appear, then, that maquiladoras will continue to play a role in the economy of the LRGV for some time to come.[36]

4.8 The Maquiladora Industry and the Economy of South Texas

It should be clear that the BIP (or MIP) and the maquiladora industry have had considerable impact on the economies of both sides of the border. Maquiladoras provide employment and fringe benefits for thousands of workers. They help sustain an economy that has long been linked to the United States. These border plants utilize banking services and transportation facilities and purchase needed goods and services in a number of U.S. border cities, thereby generating additional economic activity. In addition, "twin plants" in the U.S. hire workers, pay taxes, and buy materials.

A link between maquiladora growth and South Texas employment also exists. Between 1985 and 1990, employment on the Texas side of the border increased by 17%. Much of this change has been attributed to the growth of the maquiladora industry.[37] Studies of Brownsville and McAllen revealed that a 10% increase in maquiladora employment resulted in a 3-4% increase in employment in Brownsville and a 2-3% increase in

McAllen. This same increase in maquiladora employment led to a 23% increase in the purchase of materials, transportation, communications, construction, and warehousing services in Brownsville and a 7% increase in similar activities in McAllen. Nearly 40% of the jobs created were estimated to be with firms providing support services to maquiladoras.[38]

Virtually all imported primary materials used in the maquiladora plants come from the United States. Even maquiladoras owned by countries other than the U.S. sometimes use American inputs to lower production and transportation costs. The value of these imported goods is expected to rise to $9.2 billion in 1993.[39] Studies have shown that the maquiladoras located between Matamoros and Reynosa purchase $2 billion per year in supplies from U.S. suppliers. Of this total, it is estimated that only $2 million are supplied by firms in Texas border cities, a shortfall that should be remedied if the LRGV is to profit more from its advantageous location and excess labor supply.[40]

Some attempt has been made to increase maquiladora purchases from Texas border sources. In order for Texas to replace suppliers from the Midwest and the West and East coasts, Texas border firms must improve quality, become more reliable, and lower costs. Border communities must improve their infrastructure and provide trained labor. One South Texas study estimated that if South Texas firms could obtain 25% of the component parts and materials market, this would lead to an additional 8,500 jobs in such areas as electrical and mechanical technicians, industrial maintenance specialists, quality control specialists, tool and die makers, mold builders, computer-aided drafters, and machinists.[41]

At present, firms in South Texas supplying plastic products, paper and allied products, machine and precision machining, and chemical and allied products are able to sell to maquiladoras. Most Texas firms along the border, however, have trouble handling the large volume contracts with strict tolerance and delivery time requirements. A study of these firms concluded that modifications in existing facilities and equipment were necessary. Improvements were needed in key management areas including cost accounting, financial analyses, procurement, and marketing. In addition, it was noted that there was a shortage of skilled manpower such as mechanical, electrical, and chemical engineers; skilled tool and die makers; and experienced personnel in plastic injection molding, metal stamping, plating, casting, screw machining, and general machining. Government officials in Texas have responded to these deficiencies by providing assistance to Texas businesses seeking to supply maquiladoras with component parts and materials.[42] The Texas legislature is encouraging training programs to be implemented by South Texas junior and community colleges. Efforts to correct many of these deficiencies are underway in preparation for the North American Free Trade Agreement.

Despite the fact that many South Texas firms are not yet in a position to become maquiladora suppliers, economic benefits still spill over into Texas border cities.   For example, nearly all maquiladoras require warehousing facilities on the U.S. side of the border. Most of the foreign workers live on the U.S. side of the border and simply commute to work. Hotels and restaurants on the U.S. side of the border are used to house and entertain visiting businessmen and businesswomen.[43]   In Hidalgo county, studies have demonstrated that business travel associated with the Reynosa maquiladoras have injected approximately $27.17 million annually in the economy. As a result, an estimated 615 jobs have been created with a yearly payroll of more than $7 million.[44]

In addition to the importation of components and direct purchases of services by the plants, Mexican workers spend a substantial portion of their incomes in the U.S. with estimates ranging from 6% to 40% of every dollar earned in the maquiladoras. This appears to be particularly true of the female workers who dominate the industry. Studies have shown that as the maquiladora industry grows, Hispanic income distribution improves in the border counties with beneficial effects on spending patterns.[45] Shopping excursions across the border are not only preferred, but in many instances necessary. Using shopping passes, residents of Mexican border *municipios* may return from the U.S. with food, clothing, and other articles duty free. This is not only important to the health of the retail businesses in the border cities, but contributes to state and local tax receipts as well. This helps to explain why department stores and their parking lots are frequently disproportionately large in the U.S. border cities.[46]

Studies done by the Texas Department of Commerce have found that in the late 1980s, the economic activity associated with maquiladoras in Reynosa generated nearly $1.57 billion in annual expenditures in Hidalgo county alone. Within this same county, the 20,691 jobs in the nearby border maquiladoras created approximately 22,000 indirect positions. Further estimates have found that about 12.8 cents of each dollar entering the local domestic economy from maquiladora activity flows into the pockets of area residents through payroll earnings. This does not include the salaries of the nearly 500 maquiladora executives who live in Hidalgo county and who provide a direct stimulus of $9.18 million to the local economy. These earnings alone have generated 322 jobs.[47]

4.9 Conclusion

The maquiladora industry has had a definite impact on poverty on both sides of the LRGV border. The higher than average incomes available in the border *municipios* is a direct result of government-sanctioned, foreign-owned factories and government-mandated minimum wages. Per capita incomes in the region are at least 20% above the Mexican average.[49] The females who comprise the majority of the *obreros* are typically single and many are heads of households. Without the maquiladoras, their employment prospects would be slim indeed. Most would be forced to depend entirely on the unstable informal sector.

The economic well-being of the four Texas counties in the LRGV also depends heavily on the maquiladora industry and will continue to do so even if the rate of growth of interior maquiladoras increases. Since the service sector provides much of the employment in the region (see Table 1.3), revenue flowing from the Mexican side of the river is crucial. Retail establishments, restaurants, hotels, warehouses, financial services, and transportation services all benefit from the economic activity provided by the maquiladoras. It has been estimated that each job created in a border maquiladora indirectly leads to two jobs in the U.S., many of them in the LRGV.[50] This link would become even greater if more LRGV firms could become suppliers of raw materials to the border factories. Until Mexico is able to develop its own network of suppliers, South Texas is well-placed to serve both border and interior maquiladoras. In short, the stabilization and strengthening of the maquiladora industry would have a positive effect on poverty in the LRGV.

Notes

1. *Mexican Economic Outlook* (Philadelphia: Ciemex-Wefa, 1991).

2. E. Stoddard. *Maquila: Assembly Plants in Northern Mexico* (El Paso: Texas Western Press, 1987), pp. 67-68.

3. *Ibid.*, p. 68.

4. *Ibid.*, p. 67.

5. *Ibid.*

6. "Looking Ahead to the Future," *The Bulletin of First City Development Services Group*, 2 (1): p. 2.

7. Stoddard (1987), pp. 1-2.

8. *Ibid.*, p. 16.

9. A. Ericson. "An Analysis of Mexico's Border Industrialization Program," *Monthly Labor Review*, 93 (5): p. 33.

10. Stoddard (1987), p. 17.

11. J. Stinson, "Maquiladoras Challenge Human Resources," *Personnel Journal* (Nov. 1989): p. 90.

12. See *Maquiladora Industry Statistics* (Mexico City: INEGI, 1991).

13. M. Scheinman, "Report on the Present Status of Maquiladoras," in K. Fatemi, ed. *The Maquiladora Industry: Economic Solution or Problem?* (New York: Praeger, 1990), pp. 23-24.

14. Stoddard (1987), p. 22.

15. See L. Reyes, *The Maquiladora Industry in Reynosa, Tamaulipas: Socio-Economic Aspects* (Monterey, NL: UANL, 1988). We have chosen to use this conservative estimate. The Mexican government gives an estimate of 15% (*Partners in Trade*). Other estimates are as high as 40% (see Ericson).

16. This total could be as high as $3.4 billion, depending on the estimate used.

17. J. Patrick, "The Employment Impact of Maquiladoras Along the U.S. Border," in *The Maquiladora Industry: Economic Solution or Problem?*, p. 58.

18. Stoddard (1987), p. 18.

19. *Ibid.*, p. 43.

20. *Ibid.*, pp. 44-45.

21. *Ibid.*, pp. 48-51.

22. E. George, "What Does the Future Hold for the Maquiladora Industry?" in *The Maquiladora Industry: Economic Solution or Problem?*, p. 219.

23. Stoddard, pp. 58-61.

24. E. Williams, "Attitudes and Strategies Inhibiting the Unionization of the Maquiladora Industry: Government, Industry, Unions, and Workers," *Journal of Borderland Studies*, 6 (2): pp. 55-59.

25. B. Chrispin, "Employment and Manpower Development in the Maquiladora Industry: Reaching Maturity," in *The Maquiladora Industry: Economic Solution or Problem?*, pp. 81-82.

26. *Ibid.*, p. 82.

27. P. Wilson, *Exports and Local Development: Mexico's New Maquiladoras* (Austin: The University of Texas Press, 1992), pp. 40-42.

28. See *Maquiladora Industry Statistics*.

29. Wilson, pp. 43-44.

30. *Ibid.*, p. 47.

31. *Ibid.*, p. 55.

32. See E. Schoenberger, "Technological and Organizational Change in Automobile Production: Spatial Implications," *Regional Studies*, Vol.21 (1987) and S. Sanderson, "Automated Manufacturing and Offshore Assembly in Mexico," In *The United States and Mexico: Face to Face with New Technology*, ed. C. Thorup (New Brunswick: Transactions Books, 1987).

33. *Ibid.*

34. *Exports and Local Development*, pp. 57-58.

35. *Ibid.*, pp. 58-59.

36. *Ibid.*, pp. 59-60.

37. C. Stolp and J. Hockenyos, "Texas Under Free Trade: Some Sectoral, Regional, and Modeling Considerations," in *North American Free Trade: Proceedings of a Conference* (Dallas, TX: Federal Reserve Bank of Dallas, 1991), p. 53.

38. Patrick, pp. 60-61.

39. *Ibid.*, p. 63.

40. Texas Department of Commerce, *Texas and the U.S.- Mexico Free Trade Agreement* (Austin: Office of Trade Development, 1991), p. 103.

41. Patrick, pp. 63-64.

42. *Ibid.*, p. 65.

43. D. Molina and S. Cobb, "The Impact of Maquiladora Investment on the Size Distribution of Income Along the U.S.- Mexico Border: The Case of Texas," *Journal of Borderland Studies*, 4 (2): p. 102.

44. *Texas and the U.S.- Mexico Free Trade Agreement*, p. 102.

45. Molina and Cobb, pp. 105-112.

46. C. Dillman, "Urban Growth Along Mexico's Northern Border," *Journal of Developing Areas*, 4 (1970): p. 495-496.

47. *Texas and the U.S.- Mexico Free Trade Agreement*, p. 102.

48. K. Brook, "Patterns of Labor Force Participation in the U.S.- Mexico Border Region, 1970-1980," *Journal of Borderland Studies*, 1 (1): p. 112.

50. "Looking Ahead to the Future," p. 4.

5

Border Migration and
Economic Development

5.1 Introduction

This chapter explores the role that migration, both legal and illegal, by Mexican nationals into the U.S. plays in the economic development (or lack thereof) of the LRGV. According to federal law, two types of aliens can be admitted legally into the U.S.: non-immigrants and immigrants. The first group is made up of tourists, students, and temporary workers. The second group includes aliens permitted by federal law to reside in the U.S. These aliens have the option, if they choose to exercise it, of obtaining American citizenship after residing in the U.S. for a period of five years. This second group also includes commuters who live in a Mexican border *municipio* and work in an American border city.

Illegal aliens, on the other hand, include "undocumented workers." This term refers to foreigners in the U.S. subject to deportation for failing to obey migratory laws. Among such workers are people who entered the U.S. as non-immigrants and remained after the expiration of their visa. It also includes those working without legal documents allowing them to work in the U.S.

Some of the current problems with illegal immigration into the U.S. from Mexico stem from the "Bracero Program". Begun in 1942, this program was an agreement between the United States and Mexico to work together in an attempt to manage the migratory movement of Mexican workers. It permitted temporary immigration of Mexican farm workers to the U.S. to harvest crops, especially in the southwest where the Second World War had created a labor shortage. Mexican officials saw this program as an opportunity whereby illegal workers (sometimes referred to as "wetbacks") could be considered legal *braceros*, thereby improving their working conditions in the U.S. At the time it was thought that this program would allow Mexican workers to receive experience using advanced techniques in the harvesting of agricultural products, and that the income from foreign exchange revenue would be higher with documented workers in the U.S.

After the start of the "Bracero Program," the number of undocumented workers detained by the U.S. Immigration and Naturalization Service (INS) grew significantly. Since that time, the increase in these border apprehensions has been used as a reasonable gauge of the number of persons that illegally enter the U.S. each year. According to figures from the INS, in 1986 there were 1,671,458 apprehensions of persons who originated in and were then returned to Mexico.[1]

The "Bracero Program" ended in 1964, having allowed more than 4.5 million Mexicans into the U.S. as temporary workers.[2] In its place, the "Border Industrialization Program" (BIP) was set up in June of 1966 by the Mexican government. Mexico hoped that the BIP would create jobs in the border zone and employ the migrant workers that were continuously returning from the U.S. (see Chapter 4).

5.2 Factors Affecting Migration

The migration process between Mexico and the United States is more than a social phenomenon. In one sense, this process can be viewed as an historical phenomenon or a reclamation of Mexican territory lost in 1848 at the end of the Mexican War. More importantly, however, it can be viewed as an economic phenomenon -- a reaction to the conditions which have evolved as a result of changing economic infrastructures within both Mexico and the United States. From the Mexican side, emigration can be explained by the lack of employment opportunities, the allure of employment and higher wages to be found in the United States, and by "chain migration" which occurs when members of a family encourage others to follow over time. Chain migration is consistent with transaction cost minimization (information acquisition) and has proved highly successful for families that have adopted it.

From the American perspective, the principal cause of the migratory trends has been the increase in the demand for labor in agriculture, particularly during planting and harvesting. Recently, other industries and sectors of the economy have also increased their demand for Mexican labor. Such industries include construction, apparel, and the restaurant service industry. Within some occupations, it has been argued that U.S. employers gain the flexibility they need to compete in the global market by using Mexican labor. Such labor helps them adjust to changes in production techniques and spreads the costs of adjustment over time.[3]

Other employers actually prefer hiring Mexican labor: "Mexican aliens have a strong work ethic. They need the job; they are good workers. If you can't hire them, other workers that you might hire will be less motivated. If enforcement of [IRCA] gets tougher, then it may be hard to get motivated workers."[4] This increased demand plays a role in raising the wage differential that attracts illegal immigration. Mexican migrant workers can earn minimum wages in the U.S. as much as six times that of Mexico.[5]

From the Mexican perspective, the differences in the two economies play an important role in immigration. Table 5.1 gives a number of relevant economic indicators. As is evident, the gross domestic product of Mexico measured in $U.S. is growing but is still never more than 8% that of the United States. Inflation, unemployment and population growth remain high as well. It has been estimated that some 44 million Mexicans are classified as impoverished with workers receiving about one-eight of the wage they could earn in the United States.[6]

Wages in northern Mexican border areas also play a role in the migratory process. The higher wages in the states just south of the Rio Grande encourage migration from the interior of Mexico to Tamaulipas, Chihuahua, Nuevo Leon, and Coahuila. For maquiladoras, total wages received by workers in these plants (once benefits are included) can be three times higher than the minimum wage. During the 1980s, maquiladoras were credited with promoting migration to the border region, thereby swelling the labor pool and further exacerbating the unemployment problem. However, in a study of 800 maquiladora workers questioned about their migration patterns, 96% said they had either come to the border as children or had actually been born there.[7] Thus, it appears that other socio-economic factors play a greater role in promoting migration.

Maquiladora plants do contribute to the generation of employment in the cities, but trade and services are also important economic sectors. In 1990, 14.1% and 39.7% of the combined labor force in the cities of Matamoros, Reynosa, and Rio Bravo were in the trade sector and the service sector respectively. This compares with only 30.9% in the manufacturing sector, which includes maquiladoras.[8] In addition, many males have failed to find jobs in these factories. As mentioned in Chapter 4, most of the work available in the maquila assembly plants goes to single, young females, though this trend is beginning to change.

Studies on Mexican migratory flows point out that undocumented workers in the LRGV originate mainly from the states of Tamaulipas, San Luis Potosi, Guanajuato, and Zacatecas, especially the semi-urban, economically depressed areas.[9] These workers take temporary and/or seasonal work not desired by American citizens in the area. Some reside temporarily and others permanently in the LRGV communities, but the

TABLE 5.1

Selected Economic Indicators, 1975-1990

	1975	1977	1979	1981	1983	1985	1987	1989	1990
Total Mexican Pop.(mill.)	57.37	61.10	64.92	68.39	70.98	73.80	76.67	79.62	81.14
Employment-Inf. Sect.(mill.)	0.443	0.484	0.557	0.690	1.250	2.030	3.220	5.040	5.800
Open Unemployment(mill.)	1.750	1.790	1.560	1.660	2.250	2.350	3.080	3.030	3.270
Rate of Open Unemployment	9.8	9.2	7.4	7.3	9.2	8.9	10.9	10.0	10.4
GDP-Mexico (bill. of '80 pesos)	3370.0	3555.2	4119.9	4862.2	4628.9	4920.4	4819.6	5040.9	5236.3
% Change	4.1	3.3	8.0	8.8	-4.2	2.6	1.8	3.1	3.9
GDP-Mexico (bill. of '80 $)	88.0	81.9	134.5	250.1	148.8	184.4	141.7	210.6	238.2
% Change	22.2	-25.3	31.1	24.8	-12.8	5.0	8.9	19.7	13.1
Inflation (% change)	15.2	28.9	18.2	28.0	80.8	63.7	159.2	19.7	29.9
Mean Wage (% change)	21.3	24.8	24.2	33.4	55.8	57.7	125.0	23.3	23.1
Exchange Rate (pesos/$)	12.49	22.58	22.81	24.51	120.17	256.96	1366.72	2453.17	2807.3
GDP-US (bill. '82$)	2695.0	2958.6	3192.4	3248.8	3279.1	3618.7	3845.3	4117.7	4155.8
% Change	-1.3	4.7	2.5	1.9	3.6	3.4	3.4	2.5	0.9

Sources: *Economic Report to the President, 1991; Statistical Agenda of Mexico; Mexican Economic Outlook, 1992.*

majority of them eventually migrate to the U.S. interior where there are more industries that can offer them long-term employment opportunities. This phenomenon can better be understood by examining its history.

5.3 Historical Aspects of Border Migration

During the second half of the nineteenth century, the most important industry in the LRGV was trade, especially between the cities of Brownsville and Matamoros which lie directly across the Rio Grande River from one another. The Mexican merchant and his American counterpart sustained the small towns and ranchers, supplying most of the necessary goods. They also exported ranch products and increasingly transported goods between the extreme regions of south Texas and the bordering lands of the Mexican state of Tamaulipas. Merchants from both sides of the river joined together to provide the region with an unofficial free trade zone which they hoped would stimulate the economy. They had simply grown tired of federal government interference through the imposition of tariffs on goods imported and exported across the river. However, the wealth of these merchants was tightly held on both sides of the border and did not "trickle down" to the rest of the community. A small group of merchants in the LRGV, then, earned fortunes while the majority of the population benefitted little from their economic success.[10]

At the end of the nineteenth century and into the beginning of the twentieth century, cotton was the major cash crop. Farmers in the LRGV sent representatives to northern Mexico to recruit Mexican peasants to plant and harvest cotton for the LRGV farmers. This played an important role in the beginning of the migratory flow. Peasants were offered very high wages relative to what they could earn in Mexico.

When the First World War ended, sufficient migration to the LRGV already existed, making it unnecessary for recruiters to increase the supply of workers. During this period, the majority of land came into full production and large numbers of Mexican workers were needed to plant and harvest the cotton, vegetables, and citrus crops. At that time the LRGV was one of the most productive agricultural areas in Texas. Mexican workers came to work on farms at wages approximating one dollar per day.[11] Population in the LRGV grew in direct proportion to the number of Mexican workers who crossed the river in hopes of finding a better life. Cameron and Hidalgo counties, for example, doubled their populations during this period.[12]

The increase in the population of these counties was also caused in part by the high birth rate among Mexicans and Mexican-Americans living there. Census figures for 1910 show 226,000 persons of Mexican origin in the state of Texas. By 1930, the number had risen to 683,000, a more than 200% increase. Census figures for 1980 revealed a decline in the birth rate, though this still translated into almost five children per LRGV family, a figure double the national average.

The process of migration was interrupted during the economic crisis of the 1930s when the demand for Mexican labor diminished. However, during the 1940s, cotton fields and citrus groves once again dominated the landscape of the region. After World War II, Mexican workers continued to cross the river seeking work, many of them illegally. Farmers and growers hired them and, as a consequence, the number of arrests grew. This process continued for the next 30 years. Thus, the "Bracero Program" played an important role in promoting immigration, including the illegal kind. Many Mexicans who came as farm workers with the program became American citizens, while others did not but remained in the LRGV.

During the 1980s, the increase in the level of migration to the LRGV was the result of inflation, unemployment, and the deterioration of living conditions in those areas most vulnerable to macroeconomic crises, especially the areas that traditionally sent migratory workers to the LRGV. The perennially economically depressed areas such as the states of Tamaulipas, San Luis Potosi, Guanajuato, and Zacatecas mentioned above were particularly affected. Migrants from these and other areas in Mexico tended to come from that segment of the population with the lowest income, reflecting the lower opportunity cost of such a move. This is also true today. This same group generally has relatives and a social network already established in the U.S. providing them with lower cost information about opportunities in the LRGV and the rest of the U.S.

High demand in the LRGV for illegal labor has compounded the problem. This demand has remained strong for the past several decades and has experienced less cyclical variation than the rest of the country. Recently, in spite of contractions in the U.S. economy, the demand for labor in the service sector has increased, not only in the LRGV but throughout the entire United States. This has, in turn, increased the demand for illegal, undocumented labor. In addition to the service sector, the construction and apparel industries have traditionally hired workers without proper labor documents.

It is important to remember that almost all Mexican migrants came to the U.S. seeking work and/or accompanied relatives who were doing so. Such migration has meant that between 1970 and 1990 the population of Cameron, Hidalgo, Starr, and Willacy counties has grown at almost twice the rate of the Mexican border state Tamaulipas. Even so, this state had a combined population of more than 2 million while the four Texas counties had a population of only 701,888.

5.4 The Immigration Reform and Control Act

In 1986, the U.S. Congress passed the Immigration Reform and Control Act (IRCA) in an attempt to "regain control of the border" and decrease the number of undocumented immigrants entering the United States, particularly from Mexico. Title I of the Act makes it illegal to hire aliens who are unauthorized to work in the U.S. or to continue employing an unauthorized alien if the alien's illegal status becomes known after he/she is hired. Undocumented workers hired prior to the passage of IRCA may continue to work for the same employer but cannot change employers without authorization. Employers must request proof of citizenship or work authorization of all workers hired after November, 1986. Fines and other penalties are mandated for hiring unauthorized workers. Exceptions exist for seasonal agricultural workers as long as the employer believes that a labor shortage as defined by the Departments of Labor and Agriculture exists.[13]

Title II establishes an amnesty program for two categories of workers: those who can prove that they entered the U.S. illegally before January 1, 1982, and have remained in the country since that time; and those who can prove that they entered the U.S. legally but violated their legal status before January 1, 1982. These two categories of immigrants are eligible for work authorization and temporary status but must file for permanent residency within one year after completing eighteen months of continuous temporary status. Those immigrants who received certain forms of public assistance after January, 1982, cannot become legal residents. Immigrants who qualify for the amnesty program are ineligible for public assistance for five years.[14] It has been estimated that 2.3 million undocumented Mexican immigrants have become legal residents under Title II.[15]

The criteria for temporary agricultural workers are given in Title III. The Secretary of Labor can grant a grower permission to hire temporary agricultural workers if there is a shortage of able, willing, and qualified workers to perform the services needed by the grower and if no adverse effects on wages and working conditions will result. Undocumented workers who worked in seasonal agriculture for at least ninety days between May 1, 1985, and May 1, 1986, qualify for temporary resident status, becoming special agricultural workers (SAWs). After the passage of IRCA, over one million workers applied for legalization under the SAW program.[16] SAWs can be granted permanent resident status after they complete a one-year temporary resident requirement. An additional section of Title III allows for the admission of replenishment agricultural workers (RAWs) if the Departments of Labor and Agriculture determine that a shortage of domestic agricultural workers exist. The number of workers admitted in any given year should equal the amount of the shortage.

RAWs are eligible to apply for permanent residency and leave agriculture after three consecutive years under temporary resident status.[17]

IRCA appears to have had little impact on the magnitude of immigration into the United States from Mexico. No evidence exists to suggest that businesses which have long used undocumented immigrant labor (*indocumentados*) have experienced any difficulty continuing to do so. Undocumented workers still arrive and find work, though often in jobs that are less secure than those available prior to the passage of IRCA. Strong migration networks continue to exist since social ties span the border. Among a sample of would-be, first-time migrants from three rural Mexican communities, interviewers found that 71% believed they could find a job in the U.S. without valid immigration documents.[18] Many migrants are willing to pay the $50 or so for fake documents. As is evident from Table 5.2, the total number of Mexican workers in the U.S. labor force has continued to grow. The amnesty provisions of IRCA could be responsible for the decline in undocumented workers and the increase in legal immigrants. Thus, IRCA has contributed to a greater permanence in the Mexican migrant labor force.

5.5 Socio-economic Characteristics of Undocumented Migrants

The population of undocumented Mexicans in the United States consists of two main groups. The first group includes migratory workers who come to the U.S. seasonally and remain for a period of from several weeks to a year. These workers keep their homes in Mexico and tend to send money back home to relatives in Mexico. Contact with most of American society for this group is frequently limited to their role as workers. It is this group that is most like the *braceros* migration and subject to detainment and expulsion by U.S. immigration officials.

The second group of undocumented Mexicans consists of workers that usually reside permanently in the U.S. even though they may lack the necessary legal documents. Some of these workers have relatives with American citizenship or an approved immigration visa. Others are in the process of obtaining immigration visas themselves.

A profile can be drawn of both types of undocumented workers using information from the Mexican Council of Population and the 1980 U.S. Census.[19] The average worker in both groups is a 27 year old male. Of the first group, those that are more strictly migratory, 92% are between the ages of 15 and 44 years of age and 85% of them are male. The majority, 56%, are married, though few bring their families with them. Some 3% are divorced, separated, or widowed.

TABLE 5.2

Mexican Immigration to the United States, 1975 - 1990

	1975	1977	1979	1981	1983	1985	1987	1989	1990
A. Tot.Mex.Labor Force(000s)	17,850	19,440	21,130	22,760	24,500	26,320	28,280	30,380	31,490
B. Undoc. and Legal Temp. Migrant Workers (000s)	1,102	1,508	1,578	1,168	1,637	1,873	1,660	1,340	1,658
C. Cumm. Stock of Permanent Undocumented Workers (beg. in 1965 [000s])	972	1,187	1,460	1,620	1,761	1,961	2,225	2,069	1,527
D. Cumm. Stock of Legal Immig. Workers (beg. in 1965 [000s])	576	678	822	981	1,096	1,214	1,353	1,854*	2,534*
E. Tot.Mex. Workers in U.S. Labor Force = B+C+D (000s)	2,650	3,373	3,861	3,768	4,493	5,048	5,237	5,264	5,719
F. Mex. working in U.S. as share of Mex.Lab.Force=E/A(000s)	14.8	17.3	18.3	16.5	18.3	19.2	18.5	17.3	18.2
Remitt. by Mex. workers to Mexico (millions of $)	155	194	256	345	333	1,030	667	2,091	3,479

Sources: Statistical Yearbook of the Immigration and Naturalization Service; Mexican Census of Population; Mexican Economic Outlook, 1992.

* including Immigration Reform and Control Act of 1986.

For those in the second group, 73% are within this age bracket and 55% of them are male. Married migrants who reside permanently in the U.S. make up 42% of the group. Many of these will either bring, or later send for, their families. IRCA has encouraged the migration of entire families. In the short-run, a higher percentage of "family migrants" can pose burdens on social outlays, particularly for education.

Between 70% and 75% of these workers come from the states of Jalisco, Michoacan, Durango, Chihuahua, and Baja California, as well as from the distressed states mentioned above. The vast majority of them are from rural rather than from urban areas. The average amount of formal education among undocumented workers is about 4.5 years and roughly 20% of them are illiterate. In addition, 90% of them do not speak English. This means that their work is limited to jobs requiring little formal education and little knowledge of English. The children of these immigrants are more likely to graduate from high school than their parents, but lag in the acquisition of education beyond the high school level.[20]

According to the government survey, 72% of the undocumented workers who were sent back to Mexico had been working at least one month before their move to the U.S. The remainder had not been able to find employment in Mexico and were seeking work in the U.S. This again suggests that economic differences between the two regions play a role in border immigration. Among those workers that did have a job before migrating, 58.5% were working in agricultural sector, 15.1% in the industrial sector, and 23.5% in the service sector.

The majority of the people who enter into the U.S. illegally do so by "entry without inspection," that is without using official checkpoints. Approximately 25% of these illegal immigrants cross the border through the outskirts of Matamoros and Reynosa. Many Mexicans who want to come to the U.S. do so by employing a person known as a *coyote* or *pollero*, an intermediary who introduces and transports illegal aliens into American territory by charging a fee. In some cases, these smugglers take undocumented workers to places well within the interior of the U.S. Often the *coyote* colludes with Mexican officials, paying as much as half his earnings to stay in business.[21]

In recent years, the number of undocumented workers apprehended near the border by the INS has been growing. In 1985, 1,266,999 undocumented workers were captured by the INS. Of this number, 96% were picked up in the border area while the other 4% were found in major cities in other parts of the U.S.[22] The survey also found that 52% of the undocumented workers went to the state of California while a large proportion of the remainder go to Texas or Illinois.

Considerable speculation exists regarding the exact number of undocumented workers who illegally enter the U.S. each year. Based on the number of actual apprehensions, it has been suggested that the number of undocumented workers could well be between three and five times the number that are actually apprehended. Many of the undocumented workers seized and sent back to Mexico almost immediately attempt to re-enter the U.S. and continue to do so until they are successful. It has been estimated that some 30% of the total apprehensions involve the same individuals, therefore using apprehensions as a benchmark may bias many estimates of the actual number of undocumented workers upward.

The wages received by undocumented workers have economic repercussions as workers send a portion of their earnings to relatives in Mexico. Between one-fifth and one-third of the income in the major *municipios* comes from the U.S.[23] Table 5.2 lists the number of both legal and undocumented immigrant workers and shows that in 1990, more than 18% of the total Mexican labor force actually worked in the United States. This table also includes funds returned to Mexico by Mexican workers (remittances). During the decade of the 1980s alone, more than $11 billion was sent out of the United States to Mexico. Such sums can help alleviate a small amount of the poverty that exists in the interior of the country and reinforces the idea that much of the migration, both legal and illegal, is economically motivated. Theoretically, the focus by IRCA on permanent residence for immigrants could decrease the amount of money sent to Mexico. However, Table 5.2 shows no decline in remittances for 1989 and 1990.

5.6 Border Migration and the U.S. Economy

Since the 1970s, the number of undocumented Mexican workers employed in the nonagricultural sector has been growing. This has been attributed to the mechanization of many of the tasks previously done by manual labor. In addition, land usage has changed as more land is used for residential and industrial purposes. More employment opportunities now exist for undocumented workers in the commerce, manufacturing, construction, and service sectors. The survey mentioned above found roughly 37.1% of the undocumented workers in the agricultural sector, 24.8% in the industrial sector, and 37.6% in the service sector.

Again, the type of work done by undocumented workers typically requires little skill or training. Their jobs generally include washing dishes in restaurants, working as sewing-machine operators in textile companies, menial jobs in gasoline stations and meat packing plants, washing cars, free-lance lawn care, etc. These jobs tend to pay the minimum wage and are considered dirty and difficult. For this reason, few other workers find them attractive. The jobs undocumented workers get in the construction industry, the furniture industry, in shoe factories, as janitors in offices, and as cooks in restaurants are somewhat better paid. Employment information in the survey indicates that 30% of the undocumented migrants work in companies with less than 10 employees while 50% work in companies with less than 20 employees. Wages for 75% of these workers are less than $4 per hour and less than 2% of them receive as much as $8 per hour.

Two naive and opposing views of illegal immigration exist. One view, widely held in the last two political administrations, is that every illegal immigrant deprives a U.S. citizen or legal alien of a job. Therefore, the number of unemployed Americans will decline by the number of employed illegal aliens deported. This view assumes added importance when labor surpluses exist. At the opposite end of the policy spectrum is the equally naive argument that illegals perform jobs no American citizen would take or perform. While this may be broadly true, it is not absolutely so.

These views ignore the possibility that if low-wage immigrant labor is prevented from coming to and performing the jobs in the U.S., employers may transfer these jobs to countries with abundant supplies of low-wage labor. If this were to occur, unskilled workers in this country would continue to feel downward pressure on their wages and employment opportunities even if illegal immigration were to cease. Thus, it may well be the case that unskilled American workers are in competition with foreign unskilled workers anyway, whether those workers are employed in the United States or abroad. However, not all unskilled jobs can be moved abroad since not all outputs can be imported. This is particularly true of unskilled services. In this case, the "export" of unskilled jobs is either not feasible or very costly.

The claim that large immigrant flows harm American workers dominates U.S. policy and is reflected in our restrictive immigration policy and the consequent ongoing concern about illegal immigration. Such a claim is based primarily on a single-market analysis whereby only the effects on the low-skill labor are examined. It is a claim with merit and argues that both wages and employment levels of U.S. citizens working as laborers are reduced when immigration increases the supply of low-skill workers. If Americans employed as laborers are the target of antipoverty efforts, the influx of immigrants could frustrate such efforts by reducing the wages, employment levels, and working hours of U.S. low-skill, low-wage workers.

Even if unskilled immigrants were to adversely affect domestic laborers, it would be a mistake to conclude that it is necessarily harmful to the entire distribution of Americans as a whole. First, the immigration of low-wage labor should benefit consumers purchasing the output of this labor.

As wages are reduced and employment increases, the goods and services produced by this labor are increased in quantity and reduced in price. The actual effect of this will be a function of both the elasticity of demand for the product and the elasticity of substitution for inputs into the product.

Second, employers of low-skill labor should benefit, at least in the short run. Lower input prices for goods and services, coupled with increased quantity demanded, can increase profits. A rise in profitability will have two effects. By raising the returns to capital, it will serve as a signal for investors to increase investments (both domestic and foreign) in plant and equipment. Increased profits could also provide incentives which would increase the number of employers. The increases in capital and the number of employers will eventually drive profits down to their normal level, but as a result, the country's stock of capital rises while opportunities are created for some workers to become owners.

Third, the analysis of the market for laborers in this case assumed that the influx of immigrants had no effect on the demand curve for labor. Since the fraction of earnings immigrant laborers spend on the goods and services produced by low-skill labor may be small, such an assumption may be appropriate when looking at just the low-skill labor market. However, immigrants spend money on many products in the United States. This added demand creates job opportunities for others. Thus, workers who are not close substitutes for unskilled immigrant labor may benefit from immigration as consumer demand for American products increases.

It has been estimated that in the decade between 1975 and 1985 immigration increased the supply of workers with less than 12 years of schooling by 17% for men and 21% for women.[24] Hispanic immigrants were responsible for much of this decline. For 1980, the average immigrant had completed 11.6 years of schooling. Breaking this down, however, by ethnic group finds Europeans with 12.1 years, Asians with 14.3 years, and Hispanics with 7.0 years of schooling.[25] This increase in unskilled labor was particularly concentrated in certain cities and areas making it possible to observe wage and employment effects. Comparisons between the "immigrant cities" and other comparable cities indicate that the effects on native wages was very small, even among groups with a high proportion of unskilled labor. A doubling of immigrants, for example, produced at most a 2% decrease in native wages even when the wages of young blacks were included. Wages of women, however, actually appeared to increase by 2%. The group of workers most affected by an increase in immigrant population were other immigrants. A doubling of immigration appeared to reduce their wages by nearly 20%.[26]

Employment and unemployment effects are also small in this case. The results are not nearly as robust, however, since an influx of immigrants can cause natives of an "immigrant city" to leave. Should this happen, the effects of immigration on the employment and wages of native labor will be masked as they spread beyond the "immigrant city."[27]

It was suggested above that immigration could lower the wages of residents who were close substitutes for the immigrant labor while the real incomes of other groups could increase. Economic theory argues that if immigrants are paid a wage equal to the value of their marginal product (VMP) and are not subsidized by native taxpayers, then the aggregate income of U.S. citizens will increase as a result of immigration. This occurs because total product (the area under the VMP curve) is greater than wages paid for all except the marginal worker who receives merely the value of his/her marginal product (VMP = wage).[28]

The native-born population can lose, however, if immigrants obtain government services or payments in excess of payroll, income, sales, and property taxes they pay. Because many government programs such as public health, welfare, and unemployment insurance are primarily designed to assist the poor, immigrants stand to benefit. They are typically less-skilled and more likely to need supplemental income or support so they face a higher probability of receiving public subsidies. However, if illegal aliens comprise a large proportion of the immigrants, this probability will decline since illegal aliens are ineligible for many public welfare programs. In addition, many immigrants pay taxes, either directly or indirectly, for public goods such as roads and national defense for which the marginal cost is essentially zero. This could offset the burden of public subsidization.

The question of whether or not immigrants pay as much in taxes as they receive in public services and income subsidies has been examined. While little actual evidence exists, preliminary studies suggest that immigrants "pay for themselves" so that taxation and expenditures essentially balance.[29] Any lack of net subsidization supports the theory that immigration may increase the aggregate income of the average citizen, at least up until now. In recent years, immigrants have become less and less skilled relative to native workers. This would increase the probability that an immigrant would need public subsidies of one form or another. In addition, as welfare programs expand, there appears to be a growing awareness among all the poor of the options available to them. Thus, there is no guarantee that any past benefits received by the native population from immigrants will continue.

Studies on immigrant assimilation, or the ability to increase their human capital, have found that immigrants assimilate quite rapidly in the U.S. market. This is particularly true for groups like Hispanics which have historically begun with lower initial wages. Their long run earnings potential becomes much like that of ethnically similar natives. This trend will lessen any negative impact of immigration on productivity and income distribution.[30]

Theory predicts, then, that those who gain from immigration might gain more than the losers lose. For example, if immigrants gain from a move to the U.S. and the resident population also gains, then it is possible that the beneficiaries could compensate those who lose from immigration and still remain better off. But the advisability of unrestricted immigration would depend on three factors:[31]

(1) the possibility that anyone hurt by immigration could actually receive compensation;
(2) the probability that immigrants would remain unsubsidized;
(3) the desirability of programs designed to reduce or deny subsidies to immigrants.

Compensation to unskilled native workers for any losses received by the presence of immigrants would be fairly simple. This could be achieved through social programs such as unemployment compensation, public housing, food stamps, job retraining, and welfare payments which are already in place. If immigrants were primarily skilled, then compensation to native displaced skilled workers could be more complicated. It could well be necessary to implement special programs to ensure such compensation.

It is possible, then, for a country or region to benefit from immigration. It should be pointed out that it is also possible for the home country of the immigrants to benefit as well. This can occur if the emigrants are owners of capital and are forced by the government to leave this capital behind as a condition for leaving. Cuba, as well as many eastern European countries, have imposed such restrictions on middle-class, skilled workers attempting to settle elsewhere.

A second example applies to economies which possess a permanent labor surplus. Many Third World countries possess labor supplies which far exceed labor demand for the foreseeable future. If some acceptable level of subsistence is to be maintained, workers must leave. In this case, the home country clearly gains when workers emigrate.

A similar problem occurs in less-developed countries when high wages are paid in the urban, industrial sector. As migrants from rural areas of surplus labor flock to the cities, urban unemployment can result. Unless wage rates are allowed to fall to a level which will eliminate this surplus labor, emigration is an attractive solution. This situation obviously reflects the conditions on the border between Mexico and the U.S. It is possible that wage floors set by the Mexican government for the maquiladora workers contribute to surplus labor in this region. However, the real culprit is the lack of economic development throughout many of the regions of Mexico.

5.7 Border Migration and the LRGV

The LRGV has long had a large Hispanic population compared with the U.S. population as a whole. Since 1970, the Hispanic proportion of the population of the LRGV has grown from almost 79% to almost 85% while the proportion that is foreign-born has increased from just over 10% to almost one-fourth. During this period, the Hispanic population has grown faster than the overall Valley population (see Table 1.1). As is evident from Table 5.3, IRCA has not stemmed the flow of immigrants to this region. With the exception of Starr County, the LRGV has experienced a sizable increase in immigrants during the 1980s.

A number of immigrants enter Texas through Cameron county. Matamoros, across the river from Brownsville, is known to be favored as a border crossing point by the poorest, least educated, most rural-origin illegal immigrants.[32] Many of the immigrants who expect to be in the U.S. only temporarily remain in the LRGV, living with friends or family or building makeshift houses in the area *colonias*. IRCA limits their job opportunities, making their existence even more precarious than it otherwise might be. Those immigrants with skills and/or education who see the U.S. as a permanent home tend to venture far from the border where the social distinctions between native-born and foreign-born are more apt to blur.[33] This could help explain the low educational levels and high unemployment levels found in the LRGV (see Chapter 2).

Large numbers of immigrants can also affect the distribution of employment. Many of the jobs available in the LRGV require little education. About one-third of all jobs in the region are in the service sector. Manufacturing accounts for only about 10% of the available employment (see Table 1.6). Nominal wage levels in the LRGV have risen twice as fast as nominal wage levels for Texas since 1980. This could help explain part of the attraction of the LRGV to immigrants. It is unclear what effect IRCA has had on this increase in relative wages.

Studies have suggested that the increased number of immigrant families created by IRCA has increased the burden on education. This is certainly consistent with the pattern found in the LRGV. Table 5.4 shows that public school enrollment has increased by more than 34%. The number of Hispanics enrolled has increased even faster than overall enrollment. These figures exclude those children in private or parochial schools.

TABLE 5.3

Year of Entry for Immigrants to LRGV, 1950 - 1990

Years	Cameron	Hidalgo	Willacy	Starr
1950-59	5,109	8,228	335	796
1960-69	8,392	12,660	337	1,701
1970-79	17,789	19,939	617	5,706
1980-89	21,671	37,659	1,022	5,512

Source: U.S. Census.

TABLE 5.4

Public School Education in the LRGV

County	1980	1990
Cameron		
Enrollment	55,312	71,543
% Hispanic	87.4	92.0
Hidalgo		
Enrollment	78,126	108,251
% Hispanic	91.7	94.1
Starr		
Enrollment	8,272	11,819
% Hispanic	98.0	99.0
Willacy		
Enrollment	4,896	4,985
% Hispanic	88.9	91.3

Source: U.S. Census.

5.8 Conclusion

The Mexican government has attempted to implement policies designed to reduce the flow of immigrants by improving the standard of living and creating additional employment. In addition, the pending North American Free Trade Agreement could help solve the problem in the long run, though will have little impact in the short run. Testimony at a hearing on free trade focused on the link between the strength of the Mexican economy and illegal immigration: "We would like to emphasize that

Mexico's objective is to export goods and services, not workers...A strong and stable Mexican economy will greatly diminish the crossings of Mexican workers to the United States, consequently diminishing many of the problems experienced due to illegal migration."[34] This is a problem that has existed for more than a century and will not be solved overnight. Years are needed to raise Mexican wages and employment levels enough to eliminate the attraction that the American economy affords.

It has been suggested that migration would begin to decline when wages in Mexico reach one-fourth that of U.S. wages.[35] It has also been argued, however, that free trade might actually increase migration as additional jobs in agriculture and manufacturing are created in northern Mexico. These jobs would attract labor from other parts of Mexico to the edge of the United States, thereby making immigration more appealing and less costly. The impact of increased economic activity in northern Mexico would depend on whether employment opportunities rise faster than the labor supply.[36] If an excess labor supply exists, immigration, both legal and illegal, will continue and will certainly affect the level of poverty and economic development in the LRGV.

Notes

1. During 1990 in McAllen, Texas, 85,614 people were apprehended by the U.S. border patrol. This represented an increase of 15% over the level recorded in 1989. It is estimated that 30% of the total apprehensions involve the same individuals over and over again.

2. G. Vernez and D. Ronfeldt, "The Current Situation in Mexican Immigration," *Science*, Vol 251 (March 8, 1991): p. 1189.

3. W. Cornelius, "Mexican Migration to the United States: An Introduction," in W. Cornelius and J. Bustamante, eds., *Mexican Migration to the United States: Origins, Consequences, and Policy Options* (San Diego: Center for U.S.-Mexican Studies, 1989): p. 4.

4. W. Cornelius, "The U.S. Demand for Mexican Labor," in *Mexican Migration to the United States*, p. 39.

5. *Mexico-U.S. Fact Sheets* (Washington, D.C.: Embassy of Mexico, 1990).

6. "Resurgence in illegal immigration expected to continue," *Dallas Morning News* (Weds., Dec. 18, 1991): p. 38A.

7. E. Stoddard, *Maquila: Assembly Plants in Northern Mexico* (El Paso: Texas Western Press, 1987), p. 29.

8. *Mexican Census of Population. State of Tamaulipas* (Mexico City: INEGI-SPP, 1990).

9. R. Jones, *Explaining Origin Patterns of Undocumented Migration to South Texas in Recent Years*. (Boulder: Westview Press, 1984).

10. R. Maril, *Poorest of Americans* (Notre Dame: University of Notre Dame Press, 1989), p. 29.

11. See P. Taylor, "Mexican Labor in the U.S." In the University of California, *Publications in Economics, Vol. 6, 7, and 12*. Berkeley: University of California Press, 193-34 and P. Taylor, "Migratory Labor in the U.S." *Monthly Labor Review*, 44 (3): 537-549.

12. See *U.S. Census* and *The Texas Almanac*.

13. T. White, *Mexican Immigrant Labor: An Alternative Analysis and Policy Proposal*, Research Paper Series No. 23 (Albuquerque, NM: The University of New Mexico, 1989), pp. 19-20.

14. *Ibid.*, pp. 20-21.

15. Vernez and Ronfeldt, p. 1198

16. K. Calavita, "The Immigration Policy Debate: Critical Analysis and Future Options," in *Mexican Migration to the United States: Origins, Consequences, and Policy Options*, p. 163.

17. White, pp. 21-22.

18. "The U.S. Demand for Mexican Labor," p. 45.

19. *Survey of Undocumented Mexican Workers Returned from the U.S. Report of Statistical Results* (Mexico City: CONAPO-SG, 1986).

20. Vernez and Ronfedlt, p. 1191.

21. See Kramer, M. "Life on the Line: the U.S.- Mexican Border," *National Geographic* (June, 1985): 720-749.

22. See *Statistical Yearbook of the Immigration and Naturalization Service*, 1986.

23. C. Dillman, "Urban Growth Along Mexico's Northern Border and the Mexican National Border Program," *Journal of Developing Areas*, 4 (1970): p. 491.

24. See L. Katz, G. Borjas, and R. Freedman. "On the Labor Market Effects of Immigration and Trade." Paper presented at the NBER Conference on the Determinants and Effects of Immigration on the U.S. and Source Economies, January 15-16, 1990.

25. See K. Butcher and D. Card, "Immigration and Wages: Evidence from the 1980's." *American Economic Review*, 81(2): 292-296.

26. See L. Katz, G. Borjas, and R. Freedman.

27. R. Filer, "The Impact of Immigrant Arrivals on Migratory Patterns of Native Workers" and S.G. Bronars, "Immigration, Internal Migration, and Economic Growth, 1940-1980." Papers presented at the NBER Conference on the Determinants and Effects of Immigration on the U.S. and Source Economies, January 15-16, 1990.

28. See R. Ehrenberg and R. Smith, *Modern Labor Economics* (Glenview,IL: Scott, Foresman and Company, 1985).

29. See G. Borjas, "Immigrants in the U.S. Labor Market: 1940-80" *American Economic Review*, 81 (2): 287-291.

30. See G. Borjas, *Friends or Strangers: The Impact of Immigrants on the U.S. Economy* (New York: Basic Books, 1990): Chp. 9. A study in Texas found that illegal residents made very little use of social and welfare services, with the exception of health services. However, they appeared to pay for the health services they received. See also K. McCarthy and R. Valdez, *Current and Future Effects of Mexican Immigration in California* (Santa Monica, CA: Rand Corporation, 1986).

31. See Ehrenberg and Smith, particularly Chapter 10.

32. J. Bustamante, "Measuring the Flow of Undocumented Immigrants," in *Measuring Migration to the United States: Origins, Consequences, and Policy Options,* p.105.

33. M. Tienda, "Looking to the 1990s: Mexican Immigration in Sociological Perspective," in *Measuring Migration to the United States: Origins, Consequences, and Policy Options,* p.121.

34. U.S. International Trade Commission, *Review of Trade and Investment Liberalization Measures by Mexico and Prospects for Future United States-Mexican Relations* (Washington, DC: USITC, 1990): p. 1-16.

35. "Resurgence in illegal immigration expected to continue," p. 38A.

36. See F. Rivera-Batiz, "Can Border Industries Be a Substitute for Immigration?" *American Economic Review,* 77 (2): 263-268.

6

NAFTA and the Economy of the Lower Rio Grande Valley

6.1 Introduction

On December 17, 1992, U.S. President Bush, Mexican President Salinas de Gortari, and Canadian Prime Minister Mulroney approved a comprehensive North American Free Trade Agreement (NAFTA) as the most appropriate way to strengthen economic relations between the three countries and meet the challenges of international competition. Once it is approved by the Clinton administration, the agreement will lead to the elimination of most of the trade barriers between the three countries, including:[1]

(1) the full, phased elimination of import tariffs,
(2) the elimination or fullest possible reduction of nontariff trade barriers, such as import quotas, licenses, and technical barriers to trade,
(3) the establishment of clear, binding protection for intellectual property rights,
(4) fair and expeditious dispute settlement procedures, and
(5) means to improve and expand the flow of goods, services, and investments between the United States, Mexico, and Canada.

Such an agreement would create a trade region extending from the Yukon to the Yucatan Peninsula with a combined gross national product and consumer market larger than that of the European Community. The economies of the three countries are complementary, combining abundant natural resources, capital, and labor. If approved by the legislative bodies of the governments, NAFTA could benefit, particularly, the economies of both the United States and Mexico. Its effects will be felt directly by the state of Texas, the LRGV, and the entire country of Mexico.

6.2 Mexico's Trade with the U.S.

The Mexican Constitution of 1917 gave the government responsibility for managing and regulating the economy. The economic policies mandated by this responsibility sought a high degree of self-sufficiency achieved with substantial state intervention. As a part of these policies, Mexico restricted foreign investment, embraced import substitution, and controlled the exchange rate in an attempt to foster economic growth. The exceptions to the overall plan were the PRONAF and the BIP (see Chapter 4). With the development of abundant oil resources, it appeared that the government's policies might meet with a measure of success.

Buoyed by high oil prices in the 1970s, Mexico assumed a large amount of foreign debt. These loans financed high levels of consumer spending and unproductive investments. They also allowed Mexico to maintain an overvalued currency. By 1982, oil prices had fallen and the country owed some $86 million to foreign creditors. Painful austerity programs had to be implemented. The programs enacted decreased the standard of living, encouraged capital flight, and increased emigration.[2]

Economic performance began to improve late in the 1980s with the implementation of a market-oriented, open economy and a more disciplined public sector. A Five-Year National Development Plan was created, calling for continued stability, increased resources for productive investment, and modernization of the economy. Efforts to generate a trade surplus increased as well.

Throughout the 1980s, Mexico's attempts to restore economic stability affected her relationship with the U.S. Both countries increased their bilateral trade. Between 1980 and 1990, Mexico's exports to the U.S. more than doubled, increasing from $12.57 billion to $30.17 billion. Exports from the U.S. to Mexico also increased dramatically from $15.15 billion to $28.38 billion. The total value of bilateral trade increased by 112.2% (see Table 6.1).

This table also shows exports of manufactured and agricultural goods between the two countries. Mexico's lower labor costs have given it a comparative advantage in the production of labor intensive products while the U.S. has retained its technological lead in capital-intensive products. The value of manufactured goods exported by Mexico to the U.S. grew at an average annual rate of 15.4% between 1980 and 1990. During this same period, the U.S. enjoyed a surplus of $25.28 billion in manufacturing trade

TABLE 6.1

U.S. Trade with Mexico, 1980-1990
(millions of dollars)

	1980	1982	1984	1986	1988	1990	1980-1990
U.S. Exports to Mexico	15,145	11,817	11,992	12,392	20,628	28,375	180,419
Manufactures	11,681	9,189	9,054	10,366	17,007	24,041	145,797
Agriculture	2,468	1,156	1,993	1,080	2,234	2,532	21,209
Mexico's Exports to U.S.	12,573	15,770	18,267	17,558	23,260	30,172	215,706
Manufactures	4,374	5,331	8,060	10,443	17,250	21,236	120,515
Agriculture	1,059	1,158	1,279	2,080	1,820	2,632	18,003
U.S. Trade Balance	2,571	-3,953	6,275	-5,167	-2,631	-1,797	-35,287

Source: Committee on Agriculture. *U.S.-Mexico Trade: Report to the Chairman.* Washington, DC: U.S. General Accounting Office, 1991.

Office of Trade and Investment Analysis. *U.S. Foreign Trade Highlights.* Washington, DC: U.S. Department of Commerce, 1991.

Mexican Foreign Investment. Mexico City: Secofin, 1990.

The Interdependent Economy: Mexico and the U.S. Mexico City: FCE, 1989.

Genesis of the American Expansionism. Mexico City: ColMex, 1980.

The Politics of the Foreign Invasion in Mexico. Mexico City: Ed.Ocean, 1983.

with Mexico. Manufacturing accounts for more than 50% of all trade between Mexico and the U.S.

Agriculture, which accounted for less than 9% of all trade between the two countries, has also benefitted from the liberalized trade policies. Mexico has eliminated many import licensing requirements while the U.S. extended duty-free treatment to a number of Mexican agricultural exports. Such exports by Mexico to the U.S. doubled between 1980 and 1990, increasing from $1.06 billion to $2.63 billion. The U.S. experienced a surplus of $3.21 billion in agricultural products during the same period. Imports of U.S. agricultural products to Mexico have helped feed Mexico's rapidly growing population since Mexico's domestic agricultural production have not kept pace with her increasing population (see Chapter 1).

Texas has benefitted from the trade between the U.S. and Mexico. In 1990, the state's commodity trade surplus with Mexico exceeded $6.8 billion, much of it components for the maquiladora industry. In addition, a large part of the total U.S. trade with Mexico flows through Texas.[3] Input-output models have estimated that more than $9.5 billion in direct private goods and services exported to Mexico eventually adds some $27.6 billion in aggregate expenditures to the state of Texas. This includes $13.3 billion in gross state product, $7.5 billion in personal income, $6.0 billion in wages and salaries, and nearly 300,000 jobs. Exports to Mexico, then, play an important role in the Texas economy.[4]

With the implementation of NAFTA, trade between Texas and Mexico should increase. Table 6.2 gives projections for the trade between Texas and Mexico under the assumption that a free trade agreement is signed. Exports to Mexico from Texas could increase more than 57% by 1995 and an additional 27% by the year 2000. The projected overall impact on Gross State Product by the year 2000 represents an increase of $13.8 billion. Overall state employment could increase by more than 82% over the same time period. While these are simply estimates, it is clear that NAFTA will affect the Texas economy in important ways.

6.3 Free Trade and the LRGV

Article XXIV of the General Agreement on Tariffs and Trade (GATT) defines a free trade agreement (FTA) as an agreement under which signatories remove tariffs and other restrictive regulations on commerce on substantially all the trade between themselves.[5] This type of agreement can affect the location of industry, wage levels, employment, economic growth, and the overall economic welfare of the participants. Given the concentration of industry on the Mexican side of the LRGV and its links

TABLE 6.2
Projected Texas Exports to Mexico
($billion 1989)

	1989	1995	2000
Direct value of goods and services exported to Mexico	14.1	21.3	26.7
Indirect value, support services	23.7	38.2	48.8
Total value, all sectors	37.8	59.5	75.6
Impact on Gross State Product	13.8	21.7	27.6
Direct employment, exp. sectors (thousands of jobs)	157	232	282
Indirect employment, sup. sectors (thousands of jobs)	219	322	405
Total Employment (thousands of jobs)	376	554	687

Source: L. Jones, T. Ozuna, Jr., and M. Wright, "The U.S.-Mexico Free Trade Agreement: Economic Impacts on the Border Region." *Texas Agricultural Market Research Center Report*, 1991: p. 14. Reprinted with permission.

to the Texas border counties, any free trade agreement, either bilateral or multi-lateral, will have an impact on poverty in the region.

In 1990, the U.S. International Trade Commission held public hearings on free trade. At these preliminary hearings on a free trade agreement, most witnesses from the border regions spoke in favor of liberalizing trade:

Along the South Texas Border with Mexico, an FTA [Free Trade Agreement] could provide opportunities for both countries to expand commerce, create jobs, reduce unemployment, and increase income and retail trade. Such an agreement would certainly attract new types of industry to the region. This could help it retain many of the best and brightest of its young people, who now look elsewhere for employment. The opportunity to live and work in an area that is experiencing progressive growth should prove attractive to many, including educators and those in service industries. It should also make the region more attractive for travel and tourism and could well attract the attention of many national companies.[6]

Some, however, were not as optimistic and expressed concern about the effect of a trade agreement on displaced labor:

> Retraining laid-off workers, with the goal of making them high-income skilled workers, is often seen as the answer, but experience with such programs has been very disappointing. Most affected workers have limited educational backgrounds, and many are not young. Despite training efforts, they generally have lower incomes than in the jobs they lost.[7]

The U.S. International Trade Commission, the Texas Agricultural Research Center, and the Institute for International Economics have identified a number of sectors that will be affected by NAFTA. In each case, there are both advantages and disadvantages.[8]

Agriculture

Mexico is the second largest supplier of agricultural products to the United States. Nearly 60% of these imports enter with a trade-weighted average duty of about 7%. The remaining 40% or so enter duty free. The United States also exports agricultural products to Mexico and faces a similar trade-weighted duty on agricultural products of 11%. In 1990, Texas exported more than half a billion dollars worth of agricultural products to Mexico (see Table 6.3).

Agricultural trade with Mexico occurs in five general categories: horticultural products, grains and oilseeds, livestock and dairy products, fish and fish products, and alcoholic beverages. The demand for horticultural products in the United States tends to be highly price elastic. For those Mexican imports which face a high duty, NAFTA would lower prices and therefore increase the quantity demanded of these imports. By contrast, Mexico's demand for horticultural products is not as price elastic. A lowering of prices for U.S. goods would not have the same effect on quantity demanded. In addition, Mexico's infrastructure is currently not capable of dealing with much increased demand. Since all four of the counties of the LRGV produce cotton, corn, vegetables, and sugar cane, it is possible that increased importation of Mexican produce will have a negative effect on this segment of the agricultural sector.

Citrus, an important horticultural product for the LRGV, will be hurt by NAFTA. At present, Mexico is not a major importer of U.S. citrus products. However, competition from Mexico under NAFTA would lower citrus prices and profits, thereby hurting Texas producers and employment in this sector. Related marketing services located in the Valley would also face major adjustment as competition from Mexico increased. Fresh vegetables and melons face similar problems.

That part of the agricultural sector that produces grains and oilseeds will fare much better. The U.S. is a major world exporter of these commodities. Mexico grows very little. Therefore, the U.S. faces no real competition from Mexico in this sector. The four counties of the LRGV all grow these products and would benefit from any reduced import restrictions, particularly since they have a locational advantage.

In the livestock sector, the U.S. and Mexico export different products. The U.S. exports meat to Mexico, while Mexico exports feeder cattle. NAFTA should increase meat exports to Mexican meatpacking maquiladoras. In addition, exports of U.S. livestock by-products such as hides and skins, fats, and oils and greases should increase. Those LRGV counties with feedlot operations, however, could be hurt since they will be in direct competition with lower cost Mexican feeder cattle. All four of the counties produce livestock.

NAFTA is expected to increase Mexican demand for dairy products. Producers and processors in Texas and other border states should capture most of the benefits. In particular, suppliers of breeding stock, dairy equipment, and technical and dairy nutritional expertise would gain. Texas currently ranks 6th in dairy production in the U.S., though most dairy production occurs northeast of the LRGV.

Mexico is the third leading supplier of fish imports to the U.S. Most of these imports already enter the country duty-free so NAFTA should have little effect. The exception to this duty-free policy is tuna which will have no effect on Texas fisheries. Of the LRGV counties, Cameron has the largest fishing sector.

The bottling and processing of alcoholic beverages is far more efficient in the U.S. This efficiency offsets Mexico's lower labor costs. Therefore, it is unclear how dramatic NAFTA would be in this segment of the agricultural sector.   Texas employs approximately 3000 people in its alcoholic beverage processing industry. Only about 10% of them work in the LRGV.

NAFTA could encourage a restructuring of agriculture in the LRGV to emphasize the complementarity between Mexican products and those available in Texas. Such specialization would increase efficiency and lower costs to consumers. Clearly, some jobs would be lost in the LRGV. The effect on the overall economy of the LRGV should not be large. In 1990, 6.2% of the labor force of the Valley was engaged in agriculture (see Table 1.2). Many of these were self-employed. Only 1.1% of the labor force on payrolls in the LRGV worked in agriculture which, as a sector, represented less than 1% of the total payroll.

The agricultural labor effects of NAFTA become much more complicated, however, when displaced Mexican labor is considered. The actual structure of NAFTA excludes important migration, labor, and labor rights

TABLE 6.3

Texas Exports to Mexico, 1988-1990
(thousands of dollars)

	1988	1989	1990
Agriculture, Forestry, Fisheries	562,642	545,037	552,837
Agriculture - crops	377,328	451,006	486,189
Agriculture - livestock	174,760	63,456	47,081
Forestry	10,552	9,506	4,211
Fishing, Hunting	2	21,069	15,356
Mining	24,678	26,687	63,657
Metal Mining	7,121	6,326	3,940
Coal Mining	2,042	494	982
Oil & Gas	1,103	929	47,380
Non-metallic minerals	14,411	18,938	11,427
Manufacturing	8,483,698	10,232,765	12,487,570
Food Products	392,577	496,053	480,766
Tobacco Products	540	1,142	2,069
Textile Mill Products	179,505	199,714	256,575
Apparel	173,905	251,094	252,360
Lumber & Wood Products	40,818	55,068	64,338
Furniture & Fixtures	80,435	122,798	211,059
Paper Products	330,424	397,184	359,600
Printing & Publishing	17,057	25,557	29,160

Chemical Products	796,865	810,357	934,853
Petroleum Refining Products	75,142	318,674	323,647
Rubber & Plastic Products	413,257	363,799	448,704
Leather Products	54,941	69,684	70,819
Stone, Clay, & Glass Products	85,385	54,780	145,521
Primary Metal Industries	350,246	398,181	847,777
Fabricated Metal Products	326,399	489,338	694,045
Computers & Industrial Machinery	1,094,859	1,193,520	1,462,775
Electric & Electronic Equipment	2,946,482	3,233,488	3,249,327
Transportation Equipment	646,474	1,132,882	2,046,502
Scientific & Measuring Instruments	363,910	474,313	438,589
Miscellaneous Equipment	114,477	145,139	169,085
Other			
Scrap & Waste	263,012	206,138	183,654
Second Hand Goods	161,682	163,582	131,023
Military Equipment	56,454	8,397	7,329
	44,875	34,159	45,302
Texas' Exports to Mexico	9,334,029	11,010,627	13,287,718
Texas' Exports to the World	34,578,455	38,093,254	41,354,665
Mexico's Share of Texas' Exports	27.0%	28.9%	32.1%

IN 1990, MEXICO RANKED 1ST AMONG TEXAS' EXPORT MARKETS

Source: Texas Information System. *Highlights of Texas Exports.* Austin, TX: Texas Depart. of Commerce, 1991.

issues, though this will change with the side agreements proposed by the Clinton administration. The opening up of agricultural trade between the U.S. and Mexico, coupled with reforms by the Salinas government, will displace many Mexican agricultural workers. Unless there is considerable growth in nonagricultural sectors of the Mexican economy, many of these displaced workers will migrate to the U.S., either legally or illegally. Historically, the LRGV has absorbed many such migrants and could therefore experience an influx of migrants. This influx would exacerbate the overcrowding that exists in the *colonias* and increase the level of poverty in the region. Agricultural workers tend to be the least educated/skilled of the migrant population.

Automotive Products

The U.S. obtains many of its auto parts from Mexico which has a rapidly growing auto parts sector that is entirely foreign-owned. Chrysler, Ford, General Motors, Nissan, and Volkswagen all use inexpensive Mexican labor to supply their automotive plants. In 1989, nearly one-third of the output of the several hundred firms in this sector went to the U.S. and Canada, generating one of the largest value-added in Mexico's maquiladora industry.

Between 1985 and 1989, U.S. auto imports from Mexico rose at an average annual rate of 34%. Imports of auto parts rose by 14% annually. Trade in this sector is not entirely one-way, however. The U.S. exports auto parts to Mexico at a rate that has been growing at 16% per year. Texas shares in this export sector. Between 1988 and 1990, exports of transportation equipment from Texas to Mexico grew from $646.5 million to over $2 billion -- an average annual rate of 108%. Exports of vehicles to Mexico have been negligible because of a number of import restrictions currently in effect in Mexico.

Because of the many regulatory barriers imposed by Mexico, as well as a number of political and economic factors, Mexico's auto and auto parts industry has not become highly integrated into the greater North American automotive products sector. Many of their plants are inefficient which reduces volume and increases cost. A free trade agreement that removed many of the barriers which burden Mexican plants in this sector could increase efficiency and lower costs. It could also help integrate Mexico's auto and auto parts sector more fully with that of the U.S. and Canada.

NAFTA would not otherwise have a large impact on this sector. U.S. duties on imports from Mexico are already very low. Products produced by border maquiladoras enter at highly preferential rates. In addition, the lower Mexican labor costs would be offset by higher transportation costs. The lowering of the much higher Mexican duties would certainly make

U.S. products more attractive to Mexican consumers. However, it will be years before the Mexican market will be able to absorb a large volume of U.S. autos and auto parts. The effects on Texas and the LRGV would be minimal as well. Currently, less than 1% of the labor force in either Texas or the LRGV is employed in the manufacture of automotive products (see Table 6.4).

Cement

Much of the cement consumed in the U.S. comes from Mexico. This is particularly true in the southwestern border region where Mexican imports have captured 11% of the market. At present, Mexican cement enters the U.S. duty free. U.S. cement is not extended the same benefits, however. The approximately $2 million worth of U.S. cement sent to Mexico each year faces a 10% ad valorum duty.

Nearly all U.S. imports of cement from Mexico are supplied by CEMEX, the largest cement producer in the western hemisphere. This privately owned company dominates the Mexican industry, accounting for more than 70% of Mexico's total cement output. Production is modern, efficient, and low-cost. The company maintains extensive operations in Florida, Alabama, Mississippi, Louisiana, Texas, New Mexico, Arizona, and California.

Because Mexican cement already enters the U.S. duty free, NAFTA would have no effect on imports. Exports to Mexico from the U.S., however, should increase. This will benefit Texas which produced more than 8000 tons of cement in 1991 as well as other border states close enough to escape the high transportation costs associated with products like cement.[9] Since cement is a fairly homogeneous product, any price decrease achieved by Texas or the U.S. could certainly increase their share of the market. Currently, the LRGV employs less than 1% of its total workers in this industry. Unless this industry expands in the LRGV, the effects of NAFTA will be essentially neutral.

Chemicals

Mexico serves as the U.S.'s third largest export market for chemicals after Japan and Canada. In fact, the U.S. has historically enjoyed a favorable balance of trade in this sector with all of its trading partners. Chemical exports to Mexico from the U.S. are diversified and include primary chemicals, intermediates, and chemical products. The U.S. does import some chemicals from Mexico, though Mexico's transportation problems prevent her from being a reliable source.

Exports from Mexico to the U.S. face duties of only 4%. Therefore,

NAFTA would have little impact. Exports from the U.S. to Mexico could rise with NAFTA since Mexican duties are currently about 15%. Without this and other barriers, trade in pharmaceuticals and other high value-added products would increase. It would be possible to see a complementary increase in trade if Mexico and the U.S. chose to specialize in separate areas.

In this sector, Texas and the LRGV would not benefit a great deal in the short run from NAFTA. Less than 2% of workers in Texas and in the LRGV are employed in the manufacture of chemicals and related by-products. They represent less than 3% of the total payroll. In 1990, chemical products represented only 7% of Texas' total exports to Mexico (see Table 6.3). A long run expansion in the region would certainly be beneficial, given the proximity of Mexico and the already established market.

Electronic Equipment

The maquiladora industry dominates Mexican trade with the U.S. in electronic equipment. This is a rapidly growing sector and one of the largest operations in terms of Mexican value added. Given that most of the trade enters under special arrangements accorded maquiladoras, the effective trade-weighted duty averages only 2%. By contrast, Mexico imposes ad valorum duties totaling 16% on American electronic equipment.

Because few barriers exist for trade from Mexico to the U.S., NAFTA should have little effect on imports into the U.S. Exports to Mexico have the potential to expand in the long run if trade barriers are removed. Mexico possesses a large potential demand for telecommunications equipment, office equipment, and other forms of advanced technology equipment to enable them to become fully integrated into the world economy. The U.S. is currently in a good position to supply this needed technology which could be worth $1.5 billion. If Texas could capture as much as 7.5% of the business, this would add $112.5 million in direct spending to Texas' gross state product.[10]

The regional effect of the removal of barriers to U.S. trade in electronic equipment is likely to be small, at least in the short run. Although Texas exported more than $3 billion of electric and electronic equipment, only about 2% of the Texas labor force and 1% of the LRGV labor force are employed in this industry. Payrolls would also be minimally affected. This could change, however, if more U.S. electronics firms move to South Texas to help bolster Mexico's infrastructure and supply needed inputs to any plants located in Mexico.

Energy Products

Historically, the link between Mexico and the U.S. in the energy sector has been a strong one. More than half of the crude petroleum stored in the U.S. Strategic Petroleum Reserve has been supplied by Mexico. In addition, more than half of the Mexican demand for refined petroleum products has been satisfied by the U.S. In the last three years, exports in petroleum products from Texas to Mexico have increased at an average annual rate of more than 150% (see Table 6.3). This could increase if the state-owned PEMEX (Petroleos Mexicanos) lacks the flexibility to keep up with the rapid economic growth Mexico could experience under NAFTA.

The greatest impediment to trade with Mexico in this sector lies in the ban by the Mexican government on foreign investment in the energy sector. This is reserved for PEMEX which controls all aspects of the industry. As suggested above, production by PEMEX has not been able to keep up with increasing domestic demand and is limited by an inadequate infrastructure. Imports and exports are also determined by PEMEX and its governing board. The Mexican government, however, has hinted that changes could be forthcoming in the way these decisions are made.

NAFTA will have negligible effects unless Mexico's constitutional ban on foreign investment in this sector is lifted. U.S. duties range from zero on natural gas to 1.1% on refined petroleum products. Mexican duties range from 4.9% on crude petroleum to 8.6% on refined petroleum products. Mexico's refineries are operating at full capacity so any increase in trade from the U.S. must come from natural gas and refined petroleum products. Currently, most Mexican energy products are marketed in Texas and Louisiana.

Oil has played a role in the economy of the LRGV since fields in Starr County opened in 1929. Other fields followed in the 1930s. Total crude production for all four LRGV counties totaled almost 3.5 million in 1990.[11] The port of Brownsville in Cameron county is also involved in shipping oil through the Gulf of Mexico. Between 1988 and 1990, Texas' exports to Mexico of petroleum refining products increased by more than 300% (see Table 6.3). Despite this, the region employs less than 1% of its labor force in this sector.

Glass Products

Glass products comprise another important bilateral market for the U.S. and Mexico. The U.S. accounts for more than three-fourths of Mexico's exports in this sector, making her the only significant foreign market for

Mexico's household glassware. These products face an average 22% ad valorum duty when they enter the country. Most imports from Mexico into the U.S. are concentrated in the lower end of the market and tend to consist of fairly homogeneous glass tumblers and bowls. In return, Mexico ranks third, behind Canada and Japan, as a market for U.S. exports. Mexican ad valorum duties on glass products average 20%.

NAFTA would eliminate the high duties imposed by both countries and would, therefore, increase trade. Given the differences in disposable income between the two countries, U.S. imports would increase more than U.S. exports. This difference would be accentuated by the lack of a distribution system in Mexico by U.S. producers. Currently, U.S. investment in this sector in Mexico is negligible.

The glass products industry in Texas is quite small, accounting for less than 1% of total employment and total payment. The industry is not represented at all in the LRGV. Unless one of the large Mexican glassware companies (e.g. Vitro Crisa) chooses to take advantage of the superior U.S. distribution and communication facilities, NAFTA would have no effect on Texas and the LRGV.

Machinery and Equipment

Mexico has depended on the U.S. for capital goods for a number of years, particularly in the maquiladoras. U.S. exports to Mexico in this sector include three broad categories: machine tools, household appliances, and general industrial machinery and equipment. Ad valorum duties imposed by Mexico on these have typically averaged around 20%. Mexico exports machinery and equipment to the U.S. as well, most of it entering the U.S. either duty-free or at reduced rates that average 2%.

The U.S. machine tool industry is a world leader in custom-designed machine tools and is highly competitive in world markets. Exports to Mexico are used not only in the maquiladora industry but also in the automotive, mining, household appliance, and steel industries. In 1989, the U.S. exported machine tools valued at $101 million and imported only $2 million worth of machine tools from Mexico.

The trade in major household appliances is larger than that of machine tools. The U.S. exported $245 million worth to Mexico and imported $271 million worth from Mexico. Refrigerators, washing machines, and components produced by maquiladoras made Mexico the second leading foreign supplier of household appliances to the U.S. in 1989. Exports from Mexico supply over two-thirds of the total imports of major household appliances.

The largest machinery and equipment trade, general industrial machinery and equipment, is concentrated in the maquiladora sector. U.S.

exports to Mexico consist of pumps, pumping equipment, and industrial valves for petroleum and petrochemical production and totaled $367 million in 1989. U.S. imports from Mexico for this same period totaled $275 million.

A free trade agreement which reduced the high Mexican duties would increase exports of machine tools. As Mexico restructures and modernizes many of its industries, the demand for machine tools should rise. U.S. imports, however, should not change. Current duties are either small or non-existent and Mexico's production base is limited. Exports to Mexico of household appliances should increase as well, particularly since much of Mexico's growing population is under the age of 25. U.S. imports could expand as well if U.S. firms move more of their operations to Mexico to take advantage of the lower wage rates. In the general industrial machinery and equipment sector, the U.S. holds a technological lead which will keep the demand for U.S. products high. Those products which are labor-intensive and require only low technological skills could move to Mexico. In the long run, a general movement to Mexico could dominate the entire industry.

Texas and the LRGV may be affected by changes in this sector. At present, about 3% of the labor force works in this industry. In the short run, employment could rise with increased demand from Mexico. Jobs that were lost in the long run to maquiladoras could be compensated for with increased employment in those sectors which serve as complements to the border factories.

Steel Mill Products

Mexico accounted for about 14% of all steel exports by the U.S. in 1989, making it one of the largest U.S. export markets. These exports have typically included sheet and strip products for use in autos, appliances, and energy applications and tend to be higher value items with superior quality features. The duties on steel imports from the U.S. to Mexico range from 10% to 15%.

The U.S. also imports steel from Mexico and is Mexico's largest export market for steel. Steel imports from Mexico consist of a mix of both low-value and high-value products such as tubular products, semi-finished products, and sheet steels. Since February, 1985, these imports have been subject to a voluntary restraint agreement (VRA) which has limited imports from Mexico to less than 1% apparent U.S. steel consumption. In addition, U.S. tariffs on steel range from 0.5% to 11.6%.

A free trade agreement that removed VRAs and duties would increase both U.S. imports of Mexican steel and U.S. steel exports to Mexico. Those items such as high-value stainless and tool steel would be most affected.

TABLE 6.4

Production in Texas and the LRGV, 1988

	Texas		LRGV	
	% of Total Employees	% of Total Payroll	% of Total Employees	% of Total Payroll
Agriculture	0.5	3.5	1.1	0.8
Manufacturing	17.2	22.3	15.8	17.6
Steel Mill Products	0.3	0.4	0	0
Glass Products	0.1	0.1	0	0
Cement	0.03	0.05	0.2	0.1
Energy Products	0.5	1.0	0	0
Chemicals	1.3	2.5	0.1	0.2
Automotive Products	0.3	0.4	0.6	n.a.
Machinery & Equip.	1.7	2.3	0.7	1.1
Electronic Equip.	1.4	2.0	0.5	0.7
Textiles & Apparel	0.9	0.6	5.3	4.7
Wholesale Production	7.5	9.3	10.7	11.1
Agriculture	0.2	0.1	0.2	0.2
Energy Products	0.3	0.4	0.4	0.5
Chemicals	0.2	0.4	0.04	0.1
Automotive Products	0.6	0.6	0.7	0.9
Machinery & Equip.	1.1	1.4	0.7	1.2
Electronic Equip.	0.5	0.8	0.4	0.5
Textiles & Apparel	0.1	0.1	0	0

Transportation Services	3.6	4.1	2.7	3.6
Retail Trade	22.3	12.3	30.5	23.3
Finance & Insurance	5.7	6.9	4.5	6.2
General Services	27.0	23.6	22.4	24.9

Total Employed (Texas) = 5,452,505

Total Payroll (Texas) = $112,851,113,000

Total Employed (LRGV) = 125,576

Total Payroll (LRGV) = $1,595,445,000

Note: Figures do not include self-employed or government employees.

Source: U.S. Department of Commerce, *County Business Patterns - 1988 - Texas* (Washington, DC: U.S. Government Printing Office, 1990).

U.S. minimill producers who tend to have lower costs have indicated that they intend to compete for an increased share of the Mexican market should NAFTA be adopted. Demand by steel consuming industries such as construction, autos, and appliances would also increase exports from the U.S. to Mexico.

U.S. imports from Mexico could experience significant increases in price-sensitive steel products for construction uses such as wire products and structurals. Mexican minimills which are competitive in many product areas could challenge increased market encroachment by U.S. firms in certain areas.

On the whole, NAFTA will have only a small effect on U.S. production and employment in the long run because Mexico represents such a small percentage of the total industry shipments. In Texas, steel mill products account for less than 1% of both employment and payroll (see TABLE 6.4). There are no steel mills in the LRGV at all so NAFTA would have no direct effect.

Textiles and Apparel

The textile and apparel trade between the U.S. and Mexico has experienced rapid growth in recent years. Between 1985 and 1989, U.S. exports to Mexico grew at an average annual rate of 25%. During this same period U.S. imports from Mexico grew at an average annual rate of 19%. Much of the economic activity in the textiles and apparel industry takes place in the border maquiladoras. This reduces effective U.S. trade weighted duties for Mexican imports to 6%. However, Mexico's duties on textiles and apparel range from 12% to 20%.

Textiles and apparel actually represent two separate but complementary industries. In textiles, the U.S. possesses a comparative advantage, while in apparel, Mexico has the advantage. U.S. textile mills are ranked among the world's most productive and efficient textile producers. These mills are highly automated with the latest in technology and equipment. This increased automation has decreased employment over time, however.

Mexico's textile mills suffer from high production costs resulting from low-quality inputs, outdated technology, and capacity underutilization. The mills have also been plagued by low quality, particularly in fabric finishing and dyeing. The only competitive parts of textile production are the yarn-spinning and fabric-weaving sectors. They typically produce acrylic yarns and cotton sheeting.

The U.S. apparel industry has not shared textiles' good fortune. Unlike the textile sector, apparel production has not experienced any growth in productivity. Employment is declining in this sector and its share of the domestic market is declining. Because production in this sector is highly labor intensive and wage rates are comparatively high, many larger U.S. producers have shifted portions of their production to nations with low labor costs in order to remain competitive.

Mexico's apparel industry currently has a cost advantage of 30% to 50% over U.S. producers, particularly in cutting and sewing operations. Lower wage rates enable Mexico to remain competitive with respect to production costs. For a number of years, the industry was hampered by the poor quality of domestic cloth and the lack of marketing expertise.

The maquiladora industry has combined high quality American textiles with low cost Mexican labor to create a viable export sector. These border factories typically use not only U.S.- made textiles, but also incorporate U.S. equipment and managerial and marketing expertise. It is the operations along the border that supply Mexico's exports to the U.S. and account for much of the U.S.'s exports to Mexico in this industry.

NAFTA would continue the increase that U.S. imports of textiles and apparel from Mexico have experienced. Additional investment in Mexican export-oriented production would be encouraged by the elimination of U.S. duties and existing quotas. This additional investment would increase U.S. exports of textile mill products, at least until Mexico could modernize its own textile mill industry. U.S. exports of finished apparel to Mexico are insignificant and will probably remain so for two reasons. First, wages in Mexico will remain comparatively low for some time. Second, the incomes of Mexican consumers will limit their demand for high-priced American apparel.

Approximately 1% of the total employees of Texas work in the textiles and apparel industry (see Table 6.4) with each sector producing less than 2% of Texas' total exports to Mexico in 1990 (see Table 6.3). Unfortunately, less than 5000 people are employed in textile mills. The vast majority of the workers in this industry produce some form of apparel. NAFTA would place these jobs as risk. More than 5% of the total employees in the LRGV work in the textiles and apparel industry. Again, most (98%) of those employed in this industry work in the apparel sector. This could certainly have a negative impact on incomes in the LRGV. Most of these workers are semiskilled females with little education.

Finance and Insurance

The finance and insurance industry includes primarily banking and insurance. Mexico's 18 commercial banks were nationalized in 1982, making the government the primary shareholder. In 1990, the Mexican Constitution was changed to allow privatization of banks. Further legislation is pending which will significantly change the banking system and make it more competitive in world financial markets. However, restrictions are still in place which limit the ability of foreign banks to establish and maintain operations and provide needed capital for industrial investment.

The Mexican insurance industry is currently undercapitalized despite new laws which have encouraged privatization and foreign investment. Most insurance firms are small with limited capital bases and reserves. Protection from international competition has made many of them overpriced and inefficient. The industry is comprised of 39 firms though 7 of them control 80% of the business. Recent economic reforms have increased the demand for insurance and related services so potential for growth exists. It is expected that international competition will streamline the industry while allowing it to offer more services.

The total removal of barriers called for by NAFTA would encourage U.S. banks to expand their presence in Mexico by establishing branch banks, or in some cases, setting up separate institutions. Commercial banking presents the most attractive opportunities as economic reform makes Mexican corporate entities more attractive. Retail banking which serves individual consumers tends to require more capital investment and a larger staff than commercial banking. This makes it a less attractive alternative for early forays into the Mexican financial services market by U.S. banks. Establishing branches in Mexico could pave the way for expansion into other Latin American countries in the future.

Removal of barriers in the insurance industry could result in a significant increase in investment by U.S. firms, either through wholly owned subsidiaries or joint ventures. The U.S. industry has traditionally been more highly competitive and technologically strong. This would make it difficult for the smaller, inefficient Mexican firms to remain in the industry. Cargo insurance, auto insurance, and fire protection would be the sectors most likely to benefit in the short run.

The finance and insurance industry in Texas employs almost 6% of the population. In the LRGV, the number is almost 5%. NAFTA would give border banks an incentive to expand their operations across the border by establishing branches. Employment and payrolls for the banking sector could then increase. Employment in the insurance industry would be less likely to increase as much. Insurance is a highly automated industry and can therefore easily expand without significant increases in personnel. Overall, NAFTA could benefit Texas and the LRGV in this sector.

Transportation Services

Transportation services include motor carriers, railroads, maritime transport, and air passenger and cargo service. The government-owned Mexican railroad carries a small share of freight traffic. Foreign air carriers and ocean carriers are constrained by cabotage laws which prohibit such entities from transporting eithor persons or cargo between domestic destinations. The largest portion of trade in transportation services involves trucking, with more than 80% of the freight transported in Mexico moving by truck. Free entry into trucking in the international commercial border zones (those areas which serve the maquiladoras) is allowed by both Mexico and the U.S. In other parts of both the U.S. and Mexico, trucking is constrained by non-tariff barriers which effectively restrict commercial use of public roads.

Currently, the volume of trade in transportation services between Mexico and the U.S. is limited since each country tends to use its own carriers. At the border, it is common practice to transfer goods of U.S origin from American-owned trucks to Mexican-owned trucks. Not only does this add to the cost, but the practice has been known to cause delays of up to 15 days. Mexican railroads have their problems as well. They are beset by outdated infrastructure and procedures. In addition, a critical lack of rolling stock often causes unacceptable delays during peak agricultural seasons.[12]

NAFTA could change this, with motor carriers experiencing the greatest change. Lower Mexican wages would lead to an increase in imports to the U.S. of Mexican trucking services. In addition, the present small size and poor condition of the Mexican highway system will prevent the U.S. trucking industry from penetrating the interior of Mexico, at least in the short run. Other sectors of the transportation services industry should feel only a negligible impact of NAFTA on both sides of the border. The exception might be the U.S. airline industry which is much better capitalized and well-established, though this would call for increased investment in airports, etc. (see below).

Less than 4% of Texas employees and less than 3% of LRGV employees work in transportation services, many of them in the trucking sector. Some of these workers could be displaced by lower-priced Mexican workers as U.S. trucking loses some of its market share. This could be offset if increased trade in the border area leads to a greater demand for trucking services. If the Mexican trucking sector could not respond to this increased demand in the short run, then U.S. border trucking companies could benefit.

Retail and Wholesale Services

The retail trade provides employment for almost one-fourth of the labor force in Texas and nearly one-third of the labor force in the LRGV (see TABLE 6.4). Currently, the market area for the retail sector extends beyond the Texas border into northern Mexico. As mentioned in Chapter

4, maquiladora workers spend anywhere from 6% to 40% of their disposable income in Texas border cities. These Texas retailers either sell goods that are not available in Mexico or are not available in the same quality at competitive prices.

With NAFTA, Mexican retailers could sell duty-free American-made goods. If overhead costs were lower in Mexico, lower prices in Mexican stores would decrease the market for U.S. retailers. On the other hand, an FTA would provide access for U.S. retailers to additional products as well as to more of the Mexican consumer market. Larger U.S. retailers could establish outlets in Mexico to compensate for revenue losses on the U.S. side of the border. Several U.S. chains, including some of the discount chains, are exploring such options. With their greater marketing expertise, they would provide Mexican retailers with strong competition. Smaller U.S. retailers would be more vulnerable, however.

Residents of the LRGV are aware of their dependence on the Mexican market. Retail sales taxes make up 28% of Brownsville's tax base and 52% of McAllen's. Therefore, changes in the buying patterns of Mexican customers have dramatic ramifications for the border economy. In 1976, for example, several counties along the border became eligible for disaster relief because the Mexican peso devalution had sharply decreased sales to Mexican customers.[13]   In hearings sponsored by the U.S. International Trade Commission, several witnesses voiced concern about the negative impact NAFTA would have on some aspects of retail services in the border area. One LRGV businessman testified:

> Our local economy here depends to a very large degree upon the opposite of a free trade agreement. The fact that goods are not available in Mexico or that they're only available in Mexico at much higher prices, drives our local economies here. Our retail sales, our wholesale sales, our hotel industry to a certain extent, our tax base -- much of our employment is generated by Mexicans who come here to buy goods that are available here and not in Mexico. There's no doubt in my mind, no doubt whatsoever, that the adoption of an FTA will cut that kind of business off at the ankles and with it devastate that segment of this economy.[14]

Wholesalers account for almost 8% of the Texas labor force and nearly 11% of the labor force of the LRGV. They would face the same sort of problems that retailers face with NAFTA. In the short run, they could be replaced by Mexican firms with duty-free access to American-made goods. In the long run, the larger firms could open outlets and expand their markets in Mexico to offset any losses incurred in the U.S. Their marketing expertise could prove advantageous. As expected, small wholesalers would experience problems.

6.4 Labor and Free Trade

The focus on a "global economy" that has surfaced in recent years has ramifications that extend beyond the mere expansion of international commerce. The integration of output markets would bring about the integration of input markets as well, including labor markets. Within such a framework, highly skilled workers in advanced countries like the U.S. would benefit. The supply of these workers is limited and any increase in demand for their services would certainly bring about increases in wage levels. Low-skilled workers would not fare as well, however. Much of the world is populated with workers who possess few skills and who are willing, and sometimes eager, to work for low wages. The well-being of such workers in the more developed countries would decline.

The U.S. has traditionally used trade barriers as an important means of protection for low-skilled American workers. These workers have felt threatened by low-wage labor and have used the political power available to them in a democratic society to impose quotas, tariffs, and other trade barriers on imports. The American government has found this to be a more appealing means of income redistribution than raising direct tax to provide an increased social safety net. Trade protection has played a particularly important role in three major industries: textiles and apparel, steel, and automobiles. As mentioned above, all three of these industries have been targeted by the United States International Trade Commission as likely to be affected to some degree by a free trade agreement with Mexico.

Textiles and Apparel

Serious trade restrictions in the textile and apparel industry date back to 1957. What began with a simple voluntary agreement with Japan now includes 54 different countries and covers a wide range of products. Protection of this sort raised the prices of textiles and apparel above their free market levels, thereby increasing the demand for labor in that sector. Employment also increased in industries that served as complements to textiles and apparel, such as chemicals and allied products which supply dyes for textiles. Firms that used textiles and apparel as an input faced higher costs which were, in turn, passed on to the consumer.[15]

Changes in employment of 30 U.S. industries caused by trade protection in textiles and apparel can be found in Table 6.5. The sample year is 1984. The protected industry itself clearly benefitted with an almost 15% increase in employment. The effect would have been larger except for the fact that textiles are an *input* into the apparel industry. All but six of the

TABLE 6.5

Employment Effects in Textiles and Apparel, 1984

Industry	% Change in Employment
Textile mill products and apparel	14.95
Chemicals and allied products	2.07
Electric, gas, and sanitary services	0.14
Mining	0.10
Rubber and miscellaneous plastic prod.	0.10
Paper and allied products	0.05
Agriculture, forestry, and fishing	-0.02
Petroleum and coal products	-0.10
Transportation	-0.13
Wholesale and retail trade	-0.22
Communication	-0.26
Machinery, except electrical	-0.27
Finance, insurance, and real estate	-0.28
Stone, clay, and glass products	-0.32
Government	-0.36
Tobacco manufactures	-0.37
Food and kindred products	-0.38
Services	-0.39
Printing and publishing	-0.43
Electric and electronic equipment	-0.48
Lumber and wood products	-0.48
Primary metal industries	-0.48
Fabricated metal products	-0.51
Construction	-0.55
Instruments and related products	-0.57
Transportation equipment, except motor vehicles and equipment	-0.59
Miscellaneous manufacturing industries	-0.68
Leather and leather products	-0.96
Motor vehicles and equipment	-1.05
Furniture and fixtures	-1.88

Source: L. Hunter, "U.S. Trade Protection: Effects on the Industrial and Regional Composition of Employment," *Economic Review*, Federal Reserve Bank of Dallas (January, 1990): p. 4. Used with permission.

30 industries actually lose employment when textiles and apparel are protected. Though the percentages are fairly small, tariffs in this sector cause a transfer of income from one group of workers to another.

Steel

Protection in the steel industry centers on the Trigger Price Mechanism, established in 1978 to detect dumping by steel importers, particularly the Japanese. Any country found dumping would face increased trade barriers by the U.S. Since this policy began, levels of protection have increased to almost 30%. As protection has increased, domestic steel prices have also risen and domestic steel production has increased.[16]

Table 6.6 shows the effect on employment in 30 industries as a result of trade protection in steel in 1984. Primary metal industries (which includes steel) show the largest gain in employment. Related industries, such as mining, also experience gains though not of the same magnitude. A number of seemingly unrelated industries show very small gains in employment as well. This effect occurs because steel is an input into the production of a number of goods. As steel prices rise with protection, goods requiring steel decrease their production thereby causing an excess supply of labor. Wages then fall, allowing unrelated industries to hire additional workers. The effects are very small in the U.S. because wages are often "sticky" and labor across industries is not always substitutable. Note that the four largest losers with protection of steel all use steel as an important input.[17]

Automobiles

Protection in the automobile sector has dominated trade talks in recent years as Japan has captured an increasing share of the world market. In addition, the motor vehicle industry has been the sector most hurt by protecting steel. Voluntary restraint agreements with Japan began in 1981. By 1985, the value of U.S. automobile production had increased nearly 200% as both prices and production increased. Industry profits also rose during this period. This sector has not fared as well in recent years, though it shows signs of improvement. Under pressure from the U.S. government, the Japanese continue to limit exports to the U.S.[18]

The effect on employment of trade protection in automobiles is shown in Table 6.7. Once again, the protected industry is the main beneficiary with related industries also experiencing a growth in employment. Almost 60,000 jobs were created in the motor vehicle sector alone. However, nearly two-thirds of the industries listed lost employment as a result of trade protection for automobiles. This occurred not because automobiles

TABLE 6.6

Employment Effects in Steel, 1984

Industry	% Change in Employment
Primary metal industries	3.61
Mining	0.34
Electric, gas, and sanitary services	0.14
Tobacco manufactures	0.12
Finance, insurance, and real estate	0.11
Printing and publishing	0.09
Wholesale and retail trade	0.08
Communication	0.07
Transportation	0.07
Services	0.07
Leather and leather products	0.06
Petroleum and coal products	0.06
Government	0.01
Chemicals and allied products	0.01
Textile mill products and apparel	0.01
Agriculture, forestry, and fishing	-0.02
Paper and allied products	-0.02
Food and kindred products	-0.03
Instruments and related products	-0.11
Miscellaneous manufacturing industries	-0.19
Stone, clay, and glass products	-0.21
Rubber and miscellaneous plastics products	-0.24
Lumber and wood products	-0.27
Construction	-0.36
Electric and electronic equipment	-0.40
Fabricated metal products	-0.59
Transportation equipment, except motor vehicles and equipment	-0.63
Machinery, except electrical	-0.67
Furniture and fixtures	-0.70
Motor vehicles and equipment	-1.31

Source: L. Hunter, "U.S. Trade Protection: Effects on the Industrial and Regional Composition of Employment," *Economic Review*, Federal Reserve Bank of Dallas (January, 1990): p. 6. Used with permission.

TABLE 6.7

Employment Effects in Automobiles, 1984

Industry	% Change in Employment
Motor vehicles and equipment	6.83
Primary metal industries	1.22
Fabricated metal products	1.03
Rubber and miscellaneous plastics products	0.58
Electric and electronic equipment	0.42
Machinery, except electrical	0.20
Stone, clay, and glass products	0.18
Chemicals and allied products	0.11
Textile mill products and apparel	0.09
Mining	0.08
Electric, gas, and sanitary services	0.03
Transportation	-0.04
Paper and allied products	-0.04
Lumber and wood products	-0.06
Instruments and related products	-0.08
Petroleum and coal products	-0.09
Wholesale and retail trade	-0.10
Furniture and fixtures	-0.11
Finance, insurance, and real estate	-0.13
Services	-0.14
Communication	-0.14
Leather and leather products	-0.15
Agriculture, forestry, and fishing	-0.15
Miscellaneous manufacturing industries	-0.15
Printing and publishing	-0.15
Tobacco manufactures	-0.17
Food and kindred products	-0.17
Government	-0.17
Construction	-0.19
Transportation equipment, except motor vehicles and equipment	-0.23

Source: L. Hunter, "U.S. Trade Protection: Effects on the Industrial and Regional Composition of Employment," Economic Review, Federal Reserve Bank of Dallas (January, 1990): p. 7. Used with permission.

were an input to these industries, but because of labor market adjustments. As the automobile sector increased its demand for labor, wages
rose. With higher wages, many industries had to adjust their input mix
and decrease the amount of labor they used.[19]

Regional Effects of Trade Protection

Increases and decreases in the production of goods can be caused by
trade protection. This contributes to regional shifts in employment as
labor moves to those areas where labor demand and wage rates are
highest, leaving areas with unemployment and low wages. Employment
in the industries mentioned above is not equally distributed throughout
the U.S. Consequently, more states tend to lose with trade protection than
gain. States that have gained have traditionally been located in the
eastern part of the country, particularly the southeast. The states west of
the Mississippi have been hurt by trade protection.[20]

Changes in state employment can be estimated by examining gross state
product data by industry. If the total labor force is assumed to be fairly
constant in any given year, then absolute changes in employment can be
measured. Using 1984 as the sample year, the following states emerge as
those most affected by trade protection:[21]

Winners: North Carolina (37,000 jobs)
             Georgia (24,000 jobs)
             South Carolina (22,000 jobs)
             Michigan (11,000 jobs)
             Alabama (10,000 jobs)

Losers: California (30,000 jobs)
             Florida (13,000 jobs)
             Illinois (11,000 jobs)
             Texas (11,000 jobs)

In 1988, more than 90% of the labor force in Texas and the LRGV worked
in sectors that did not directly benefit from trade protection.

Effects of NAFTA

In a fully employed economy, trade liberalization would eliminate the
distortions mentioned above, but it would have little effect on the overall
level of employment. The last few years have seen less than full
employment in the U.S. so NAFTA would exacerbate the problem. In
addition, NAFTA can affect wage levels and immigration.

Relative wages in two countries engaged in trade liberalization change as the price of tradeable goods begins to equalize. When product prices equalize, factor prices (or prices of inputs), including wages, will equalize as well either through worker migration or labor services embodied in goods. In the case where product prices fail to converge, wage gaps may not converge either, but the gap will narrow.

In a model developed by the staff of the U.S. International Trade Commission, estimates were made of the medium-term effect of trade liberalization on real wages for skilled and unskilled workers in the U.S. and Mexico. Preliminary results suggest that the wage differential will narrow with the largest part of the adjustment occurring in Mexico. In addition, with increasing wages in Mexico, migration to the U.S. would decline. This, in turn, would lead to reduced expenditures on border control, education, and social services.[22]

The effects of this narrowing of the wage gap could be different for skilled and unskilled workers. The real income of skilled workers would rise since Mexican exports rely more heavily on unskilled labor than do Mexican nontraded goods. In contrast, the real income of unskilled workers would fall slightly. The fact that less than 50% of the population of the LRGV age 25 years and older are high school graduates places them at risk. Many of the jobs in this area are predominantly unskilled. Service sector jobs that cannot be exported will not be as affected as agricultural and manufacturing jobs. In a broader context, however, total real income in both countries could increase because of the trade-creating benefits of NAFTA.[23] At the very least, the attention caused by NAFTA will encourage governments at both the state and national level to allocate resources for socioeconomic issues that might affect trade.

6.5 Infrastructure Needs of the LRGV

Between 1980 and 1990, the population of the counties comprising the LRGV grew at an average annual rate of 3.1% while the three largest *municipios* on the Mexican side of the border increased at an average annual rate of 2.6% (see Tables 1.1 and 1.8). Brownsville and McAllen appeared on lists of the fastest growing metropolitan areas during the 1980s.[24] The growth of urban areas to accommodate these increasing numbers has, in many cases, failed to provide adequate services (see Chapter 3). Water is becoming an increasingly scarce resource despite the proximity to the Rio Grande River. Sewer systems and municipal waste plants are needed to handle the wastes being generated. Urban growth will certainly not decrease with NAFTA. Development plans for the area must include essential services for the growing population.

Trade has also increased in the border area. Between 1988 and 1990, the U.S.'s exports to Mexico increased by 87% while Mexico's exports to the U.S. increased by 140%. Mexico became a member of the General Agreement on Tariffs and Trade (GATT) in 1986 and is now the U.S.'s third largest trading partner. Accordingly, commercial traffic has increased during this period, placing a strain on the existing facilities. A free trade agreement which further decreases trade barriers will exacerbate the problems which currently exist.

At the Hidalgo border crossing linking McAllen and Reynosa, more than 128,000 freight carriers and approximately 13.6 million people crossed the border in 1989. A large portion of truck shipments from Mexico into the U.S. enter here, yet no major interstate highway exists to service this traffic nor is there a Class 1 rail line. This poses unacceptably high maintenance expenditures on Hidalgo county. McAllen's Miller International Airport also handles a high level of cargo, thereby increasing the strain on the maintenance budget.[25]

In the Brownsville-Matamoros metropolitan area, the infrastructure faces similar burdens. A significant number of northbound truck shipments and southbound rail shipments go through this region. Federal Highway 77 and the Union Pacific and Southern Pacific rail lines bear much of this traffic. Maintenance expenditures for Cameron county are among the region's highest. Brownsville is also a port which handles an increasing amount of foreign commerce. Projects to update port facilities and deepen the channel are underway.[26]

Exporters who testified before the U.S. International Trade Commission hearings felt that the overburdened U.S. infrastructure in the border area hindered their access to the Mexican market. They argued that inadequacies existed in the following areas: U.S. highways in the border region, railroad capacity crossing into Mexico, and the existing customs facilities. These inadequacies frequently contributed to shipment delays of several days.[27] One hearing participant noted that "there seems to be a lack of appreciation on the part of Federal agencies involved on the need not only to construct new facilities, but to revisit established border stations to determine better ways to improve the physical access of passenger and commercial vehicles."[28]

Maquiladora growth has also contributed to the infrastructure problems. Between 1989 and 1990, the number of plants in the LRGV section of Tamaulipas increased by 30% with an additional 11% increase the following year. This growth has contributed to the population growth and trade increase. It has also added to the burden which already exists on water and sewer systems.

TABLE 6.8

Tourism Expenditures for the U.S. and Mexico, 1980-1990
(billions of dollars)

	1980	1981	1982	1983	1984	1985	1986	1987	1988	1989	1990
Total Exp. in Mexico	5.39	6.53	2.64	2.73	3.28	2.90	2.99	3.50	4.00	4.77	5.33
Interior	1.67	1.76	1.40	1.63	1.95	1.72	1.79	2.27	2.54	2.96	3.40
Border	3.72	4.77	1.24	1.10	1.33	1.18	1.20	1.23	1.46	1.81	1.93
Total Exp. in U.S.	4.17	6.16	2.21	1.58	2.17	2.26	2.18	2.37	3.20	4.25	5.38
Interior	1.04	1.57	0.79	0.44	0.65	0.66	0.62	0.78	1.11	1.55	1.94
Border	3.13	4.59	1.43	1.14	1.52	1.60	1.56	1.59	2.09	2.70	3.44

Source: *Mexican Economic Outlook.* Bala Cynwyd, PA: Economic Research Center About Mexico, 1992.

Tourism has also played a role in the economic activity of the region. Table 6.8 provides information on tourism expenditures for both Mexico and the U.S. In 1980, U.S. citizens spent $5.39 billion in Mexico. More than half of this was spent in the border area. Ten years later, U.S. citizens were still spending a little over $5 billion, but only 36% of it was spent in the border area. Mexican tourists, however, spent far more in the border area of the U.S. In 1980, 84% of a total of $3.7 billion dollars was spent on the border. By 1990, border spending was still 73% of $5.38 billion. Border spending could increase in the near future. The Los Caminos del Rio Heritage Project, created in 1990, has been working to heighten public awareness of the region's historic sites. A number of sites on both sides of the Rio Grande have been targeted as landmarks with the hope that community pride will contribute to economic development. A "Northern Border Program" has been implemented by Mexico which will allow foreign buses to cross the border, thereby attracting even more visitors.[29] This kind of activity, however, poses additional strains on the infrastructure of the border area.

Attempts have been made to systematically identify the infrastructure needs of the region. Airports, educational facilities, health care facilities, surface transportation, ports, and water and sewage have all been targeted. In 1991, $375 million in federally funded projects were proposed for Brownsville while $394 million worth of projects were proposed for the McAllen area (see Table 6.9). The majority of these funds were targeted specifically for transportation. Unfortunately, these funds failed to be fully allocated, leaving much to be done to meet important infrastructure needs of the region. Recently, Mexico's Social Development Secretariat has allocated funds for the cities of Matamoros and Reynosa in an attempt to improve industrial and social infrastructure.[30]

The Texas Legislature has also expressed concern over various aspects of border infrastructure. At their request, the Texas/Mexico Authority, a private sector advisory body to the Texas Department of Commerce, conducted a study to explore the impact of a free trade agreement on the Texas economy. This group's recommendations on the infrastructure included:[31]

- increased funding to accommodate traffic in the border region
- continued funding for the Texas Centers for Border Economic and Enterprise Development
- creation of a series of Bi-National Skill and Technology Institutes along the Texas-Mexico border to improve worker skills
- creation of new ports of entry to promote new trade opportunities
- extension of in-state tuition allowance to Mexican students enrolled in Texas border junior and community colleges

TABLE 6.9

Infrastructure Projects for the LRGV, 1991
(millions of dollars)

	Brownsville	McAllen-Pharr
Airports	12.4	20.0
Education/Tech. Transfer	20.6	3.0
Environment	41.0	5.0
Health Care	15.5	0
Housing	25.0	1.8
Ports of Entry	77.3	44.0
Surface Transportation	150.5	300.0
Water and Sewer	32.5	20.0
Total	374.8	393.8

Source: D. Mitchie, *An Industrialization Program for the Texas-Mexico Border*. El Paso: Institute for Manufacturing and Materials Management, 1991.

· development of a joint teacher certification program to increase standards at the primary and secondary levels in the border region
· increased funding for the Texas Water Development Board for use in economically depressed areas
· assessment of housing needs in the border region along with water, sewage, and waste management
· construction of a hydro-electric dam on the Texas-Mexico border with revenues generated by the project to be utilized for environmental improvement
· continued improvement of transborder telecommunication services
· further development of water port facilities and deep containerization facilities at ports handling border commerce
· bi-national efforts to substantially improve health care activities and facilities in the border area
· a program to increase the awareness of customs officials as the needs and concerns of individuals crossing the border

The adoption of many, if not all, of the recommendations would eliminate most of the constraints currently imposed by the border infrastructure. It will also increase the geographical advantage of the U.S.- Mexico border and allow more people to live in a Texas border city while working on the Mexican side of the border.

6.6 NAFTA and the Environment

Environmental issues have plagued Congressional debate on NAFTA, though neither Canada nor Mexico feel that environmental questions belong in the text of a trade agreement. Three concerns appear to dominate the debate in the U.S.:[32]

(1) There is a fear that increased industrialization will strain the environmental infrastructure;
(2) The U.S. and Canada worry that they will be unable to compete with Mexican firms who face less expensive and comprehensive pollution standards;
(3) Many argue that NAFTA might directly and indirectly weaken environmental standards within the U.S. as Mexico pollutes the water and air along the border.

These concerns have prompted suits from environmental groups and resolutions in Congress which thus far have had little impact on the progress of NAFTA. The Clinton administration has pledged to deal with these issues.

Mexico has also been concerned about environmental issues. President Salinas' government has passed a number of measures designed to protect the environment. Environmental impact studies must now be filed by new firms and the number of environmental inspectors has more than tripled, especially in the border region. Several hundred plants have been shut down along the border for violating Mexican environmental laws. Despite these attempts to address the problem, strong enforcement of the increasingly stringent relations appears to be lacking.[33]

Environmental issues compound the issues facing the LRGV and have been the source of many complaints from critics of NAFTA. As mentioned in Chapter 3, the area has long suffered from the contaminated drinking water, poor sewage treatment, and polluted rivers caused, in part, by the *colonias* on both sides of the border. The presence of maquiladoras has increased unauthorized hazardous waste dumps, reduced air quality, and placed a strain on municipal services. Clearly, these issues must be addressed if NAFTA is to enhance economic development in the LRGV.

6.7 Conclusion

It is difficult to accurately predict the total impact free trade will have on the economy of the LRGV. Many of the details remain to be worked out between the countries involved. In addition, a number of provisions will be phased in over a number of years, tempering any negative effects that might occur. Certainly this part of Texas is well-placed to integrate itself fully into Mexico's low-cost labor sectors. Further, the Valley already has access to U.S. markets and possesses an efficient transportation sector. This should firmly establish the Valley's role as a globally competitive production-sharing site.

The transformation will not be without its costs. Labor in the LRGV must adapt. This may not be easy since many who make up the labor force are low-skilled and service-oriented. If there is a long phase-in period as currently proposed, adjustment will be easier. Jobs which complement maquiladora production (i.e. textiles) could move to the border.

Capital-intensive, high-value-added production should actually gain with NAFTA. The number of joint ventures between producers in Texas and Mexico could increase as well, capitalizing on one another's respective comparative advantages. Border locations will continue to be attractive to firms seeking close proximity and low transportation costs. In short, NAFTA will increase economic activity along the Texas side of the border, thereby drawing attention to the problems that currently exist.

NAFTA will cause changes within the maquiladora industry. In fact, it has been argued that the implementation of a free trade agreement will be "the beginning of the end" of the industry.[34] The benefits currently accorded the maquiladoras will extend to all industries and the maquiladoras will be able to sell their products within Mexico. With the loss of special treatment, there will be less incentive for new maquiladoras to locate on the border. If the current maquiladoras remain along the border, this should not have much of a negative impact on the LRGV. A recent survey of border maquiladoras found that two-thirds of the existing plants did not plan to relocate.[35] Thus, unemployment would not necessarily rise, nor would spending the Valley necessarily decrease. It could even prove beneficial if it decreased migration from the interior of Mexico to the border. A slowing of the growth of border maquiladoras should also temper the environmental problems which currently exist.

The Clinton administration has pledged to support NAFTA. On August 13, 1993 negotiators from the U.S., Canada, and Mexico completed supplemental agreements on the environment, labor, and import surges. These agreements create a trinational commission to not only deal with these important issues, but to mediate disputes between the three countries as well. The commission would have the authority to refer all disputes to an arbitration panel of independent experts. Parties found guilty of violations of the treaty would be subject to trade sanctions and/or fines.

According to the supplemental agreement, the U.S. and Mexico agree to finance improvements in the environment and infrastructure along the polluted Texas-Mexico border, though specific details were not provided. Current environmental laws would be enforced with penalties incurred by violators. The commission was empowered to receive environmental complaints and to advise on environmental issues. Policymakers have pledged to ensure high environmental standards though environmental protection groups remain skeptical.

As a part of the agreement on labor, Mexico has agreed to work to raise minimum wages paid to Mexican workers, linking them to productivity increases in hopes of improving the standard of living in Mexico. In addition, basic guarantees protecting workers' rights, prohibiting child labor, ensuring health and safety standards, and promoting industrial relations were put in place. Though labor leaders in the U.S. have not been supportive of NAFTA, the Clinton administration has estimated that an additional 200,000 jobs will be created.

These supplemental agreements have sparked much debate, but could appease some of the many current U.S. critics of NAFTA and help speed passage through Congress. In the short run, NAFTA will require adjustments throughout the economy. However, if programs are in place to adapt to the expanding trade opportunities, then the LRGV could experience a decrease in the level of poverty as economic development progresses. Without such development, the prospects for the region remain bleak.

Notes

1. See G. Hufbauer and J. Schott, *North American Free Trade: Issues and Recommendations* (Washington, DC: Institute for International Economics, 1992).

2. United States International Trade Commission, *The Likely Impact on the United States of a Free Trade Agreement with Mexico* (Washington,DC: USITC, 1991),p. 1-1.

3. L. Jones, T. Ozuna, Jr., and M. Wright, "The U.S.-Mexico Free Trade Agreement: Economic Impacts on the Border Region," *TAMRC International Market Research Paper no. IM-16-91* (College Station, TX: Texas A&M University, 1991), p.4.

4. *The Impact of Mexican Trade on the Texas Economy* (Waco, TX: Perryman Consultants, Inc., 1991), p.19.

5. *Ibid.*, p. xix.

6. United States International Trade Commission, *Review of Trade and Liberalization Measures* (Washington, DC: USITC, 1991), p.1-14.

7. *Ibid.*, p. 1-20.

8. The following information is, in large part, a summary of several publications prepared by the U.S. International Trade Commission, the Institute for International Economics, and Texas A&M University. For more detail, see *The Likely Impact on the United States of a Free Trade Agreement with Mexico, Review of Trade and Investment Liberalization Measures by Mexico and Prospects for Future, NAFTA: An Assessment, North American Free Trade: Issues and Recommendations,* and numerous publications by the Texas Agricultural Market Research Center at Texas A&M University.

9. Dallas Morning News. *Texas Almanac 1992-93* (Houston: Gulf Publishing Co., 1991), p. 618.

10. *The Impact of Mexican Trade on the Economy,* p. 20.

11. *Texas Almanac,* pp. 613-614.

12. *Review of Trade and Liberalization Measures,* pp. 2-20 - 2-21.

13. S. Weintraub and L. Boske. *U.S.- Mexico Free Trade Agreement: Economic Impact on Texas* (Austin: LBJ School of Public Policy, 1992), pp. 68-69.

14. Quoted in *Review of Trade and Investment Liberalization Measures,* pp.1-21-1-22.

15. L. Hunter, "U.S. Trade Protection: Effects on the Industrial and Regional Composition of Employment," *Economic Review* (Jan. 1990): pp. 2-3.

16. *Ibid.,* p. 5.

17. *Ibid.,* pp. 5-6.

18. *Ibid.,* pp. 7-8.

19. *Ibid.,* pp. 7-9.

20. *Ibid.,* pp. 9-11.

21. *Ibid.,* p. 11.

22. *The Likely Impact of a Free Trade Agreement with Mexico,* pp. 25-26.

23. *Ibid.*

24. S. Cobb and D. Molina, "Implications of North American Free Trade for Infrastructure and Migration on the Texas-Mexico Border," in *North American Free Trader: Proceedings of a Conference* (Dallas: Federal Reserve Bank of Dallas, 1991): p. 78.

25. *Ibid.,* pp. 79-80.

26. *Ibid.,* p. 80.

27. *Review of Trade and Investment Liberalization Measures,* pp. 1-2 - 1-3.

28. Quoted in *Review of Trade and Investment Liberalization Measures,* pp. 1-21 - 1-22.

29. "Foreign and Mexican Capital of $10 billion to Expand Mexico's Vibrant Tourism Industry," *Wall Street Journal* (October 1, 1990): B12.

30. See *Protecting the Environment: Mexico's Public Works Program for the Border Region* (Mexico City: Secretariat of Social Development, 1992).

31. See Texas Department of Commerce, *Texas and the U.S.- Mexico Free Trade Agreement* (Austin: Office of Trade Development, 1991).

32. *North American Free Trade: Issues and Recommendations,* pp. 132-33.

33. G. Hufbauer and J. Schott, *NAFTA: An Assessment* (Washington, DC: Institute for International Economics, 1993), pp. 91-92.

34. *North American Free Trade: Issues and Recommendations*, p. 334.

35. *U.S.- Mexico Free Trade Agreement: Economic Impact on Texas*, p. 81.

7

Problems and Prospects: A Summary

7.1 Introduction

It should now be evident that the analysis of socio-economic conditions on the Mexico-Texas border is a study involving remarkable contrasts. The level of poverty and degree of general economic despair in the border region should be apparent to even the most casual observer. What is perhaps not as obvious is the tremendous economic potential of the region. We have attempted to show that the problems of the LRGV are many-faceted. They have cultural and historical roots that must be accounted for when proposing solutions. Failure to recognize and address all dimensions of the existing problems will limit the effectiveness of any proposed remedies.

7.2 Problems in the LRGV

Part of the economic problems that exist on the border are a consequence of demographic change. Many of these demographic variables are beyond the control of governments or policymakers. It is unlikely that the population growth rate or the age distribution within the population will change in the foreseeable future. Any strategy or set of strategies must understand this point. However, the problems of unemployment, low education levels, and job opportunities can be addressed by appropriate policies. This would, in turn, raise the low levels of per capita income in the region. The overview provided in Chapter 1 should make the nature of the demographic characteristics clear.

The second chapter of the book attempted to illustrate the difficulty of quantifying many of the socio-economic problems of the border region. Any discussion of poverty requires, first of all, a careful definition of the term. This was provided along with a description of the poverty that exists in northeastern Mexico and South Texas and the policies that have been implemented in an attempt to alleviate the problems in these areas. A brief look at current figures, however, makes it clear that the many so-called "Great Society" programs currently in place have not had stellar results. Unemployment in 1990 was still more than twice the national average, making median family incomes almost half the national average. More than 40% of the population of the LRGV is considered to be living in poverty.

Chapter 3 explained and discussed in detail one of the physical manifestations of the border problems, the *colonias* which blight the area. These pockets of poverty house nearly 17% of the population in the LRGV and are characterized by substandard housing, inadequate sanitation and water facilities, low education levels, and a Third World disease environment. Government efforts at all levels have merely contained the problem. Before social and economic development in the LRGV can take place, the problems of the *colonias* must be corrected, not just contained.

In Chapter 4, attention is paid to the role of economic growth and development in eliminating the poverty and unemployment problems on both sides of the border. At present, the maquiladora industry is the "primary engine of economic growth" in this region. The chapter discusses the impact of the industry on a number of different sectors. We show that maquiladoras not only provide direct employment for thousands of workers on both sides of the border, but have indirect effects as well. Banking, transportation, services, and the retail sector of U.S. border cities all benefit. Clearly, the economic well-being of the LRGV depends heavily on the maquiladora industry. Estimates indicate that each job created in a border maquiladora leads to two jobs in the U.S., many of them in the LRGV. Maquiladoras, then, play a prominent role in the alleviation of poverty and the long run economic development of the region.

Chapter 5 provided a comprehensive discussion of the migration issue. The flow of human capital from both sides of the Mexico-Texas border has long been the source of considerable debate. This debate has been both public and acrimonious. Most individuals feel strongly that either all migration from Mexico to the U.S. should be stopped, or that the border floodgate should be opened. We have attempted to show that economic theory, as well as economic reality, fails to support the catastrophic predictions of job losses by Americans to both legal and illegal immigrants. U.S. citizens typically refuse to accept many of the relatively low-skill, low-wage jobs available. Thus, we have a segmented labor market that limits competition between immigrants and non-immigrants. Any meaningful discussions of the job creation/job loss implications of more open international labor markets must address the differences between the various forms of labor that do actually cross the border.

Finally, Chapter 6 discusses perhaps the most realistic hope for curing the ills that afflict the LRGV, the North American Free Trade Agreement. Given the concentration of industry on the Mexican side of the Rio Grande River and the links to the Texas border counties, any agreement that stimulates trade and investment will affect the level of poverty in the area. As economic activity increases, the border region can easily integrate itself into Mexico's low-cost labor sectors. Current business patterns already allow for access to U.S. markets, complete with an efficient transportation sector. Labor, however, will have to adjust. Training will be needed to integrate the Valley labor force more fully into the growing maquiladora industry and its offshoots. As firms move closer to Mexico, the LRGV should benefit from the economic growth and development that will occur with such a move.

7.3 Strategies for a Brighter Future

The many problems that plague the LRGV can be addressed, though not perhaps at once. As increasing attention has been focused on the region, various task forces sponsored by government agencies and private organizations have proposed a number of solutions, many of which have been mentioned in the previous chapters. Some of these solutions address the more immediate social and economic concerns. Most, however, recognize the need for long-term growth and development. Strategies for change have been put forward in three broad categories.

Socio-economic Development

· Make affordable health care available to all residents, regardless of ability to pay
· Use physicians' assistants and other para-medical personnel to decrease waiting times at local clinics and hospitals
· Educate residents about proper inoculation, general preventative health measures, pregnancy prevention, and other health issues
· Expand the federal government's WIC program to lower the infant mortality rate for the region
· Expand care facilities for the indigent elderly and disabled
· Develop programs to eliminate malnutrition
· Upgrade LRGV school districts, both in terms of physical plant and curriculum
· Develop programs to help parents assist their children in succeeding in school
· Provide incentives to students to remain in school
· Develop programs to eliminate illiteracy at all ages

- Increase federal spending for Head Start programs
- Increase federal spending for Project Development Continuity
- Create a series of Bi-National Skill and Technology Institutes along the Texas-Mexico border to improve worker skills
- Extend in-state tuition allowances to Mexican students enrolled in Texas border junior and community colleges
- Develop a joint teacher certification program to increase standards at the primary and secondary levels in the border region
- Provide help to female heads of households by providing child care and job training
- Adopt income subsidies based on need rather than labor force status
- Implementation of either a negative income tax or negative wage tax to restore incentives to work
- Develop a program to increase the awareness of custom officials of the needs and concerns of individuals crossing the border
- Develop a comprehensive job training program tied to public works that would not only increase skill levels but help improve the infrastructure

Economic Development

- Increase job opportunities for females, particularly in Starr and Willacy counties
- Enforce legislation to eliminate discrimination
- Support the implementation of the North American Free Trade Agreement, which could provide jobs in border counties
- Develop retraining programs to ease the adjustment of low-skill workers to a free trade agreement
- Improve the quality, reliability, and cost structure of border suppliers of maquiladoras
- Help strengthen the Mexican economy to reduce the wage gap between the two countries
- Provide government assistance to Texas businesses seeking to supply maquiladoras
- Continue funding for the Texas Centers for Border Economic and Enterprise Development
- Develop a comprehensive economic development plan for the border region
- Continue support for the Los Caminos del Rio Heritage Project to promote tourism in the region

Physical Development

- Develop plans for environmental conservation of both sides of the border
- Establish a $500 million pool for the development of water and sewers in the *colonias*
- Provide a series of grants and low-interest loans to families for connection to sewer systems
- Increase appropriations of Community Development Block Grant funds for cities and other government entities affected by *colonias*
- Develop alternative affordable housing options
- Provide grants or low-interest loans for domestic utility hook-ups, with funding to be earmarked specifically for residents whose income level is below minimum income levels designated for currently existing programs
- Develop programs to help residents of the border region find new construction funds administered through existing housing assistance programs with income level requirements below current FHA limitations
- Continued federal support of funding programs geared towards building and expanding public, private, and mutual domestic sewer and water systems
- Federal investigation into and support of methods of addressing illegal subdivisions
- Increased funding to accommodate traffic in the border region
- Increased funding for the Texas Water Development Board for use in economically depressed areas
- Construction of a hydro-electric dam on the Texas-Mexico border with revenues generated by the project to be utilized for environmental improvement
- Continued development of transborder telecommunication services
- Further development of water port facilities and deep containerization facilities at ports handling border commerce
- Creation of new ports of entry to promote trade opportunities

Clearly, all of these proposed solutions are costly. The issue becomes one of time. These problems can be addressed now, and costs can be incurred now to solve them. If this not done, the pecuniary and human costs that will be faced in the future will be enormous.

7.4 Conclusion

The United States and Mexico are both faced with crises that permeate all segments of society. The crisis that currently exists in the Lower Rio Grande Valley is unique, consisting of demographic, socio-economic, and economic conditions that are unlike other regions of either country. For this reason, the two countries must work together to resolve the problems that exist. Every effort must be made to develop a bi-national plan for social and economic development that will meet both the short-term and long-term goals mentioned throughout this study. Success in resolving the problems of the region will strengthen both countries and truly make the Lower Rio Grande Valley "a Magic Valley."

Selected Bibliography

A Partnership for Growth. Washington, DC: Department of Commerce, 1990.

Acuña, R. *Occupied America: A History of Chicanos, 2nd. Ed.* New York: Harper and Row, 1981.

Allen, S. Testimony before the U.S. House of Representatives Select Committee on Public Works and Transportation, March 12, 1988.

Alm. R. "Clinton's NAFTA Strategy." *The Dallas Morning News.* (Monday, March 29, 1992): 1D.

Applegate, H. Testimony before the U.S. House of Representatives Select Committee on Public Works and Transportation, March 12, 1988.

A Review of Head Start Research Since 1970. Washington, DC: U.S. Department of Health and Human Services, 1983.

Aspe, P. and J. Beristain. *Distribution of Education and Health Opportunities and Services.* New York: Holmes and Meier Publishers, Inc., 1984.

Baerrensen, D. "Unemployment and Mexico's Border Industrialization Program." *Inter-American Economic Affairs,* 29 (2): 79-90.

Barrero, M. *Race and Class in the Southwest: A Theory of Racial Inequality.* Notre Dame: Notre Dame University Press, 1979.

Bath, C. "Environment: U.S. Perspective." In *U.S.- Mexican Industrial Integration: The Road to Free Trade.* Ed. S. Weintraub. Boulder: Westview Press, 1990.

Bean, F., A. King, and J. Passel. "Estimates of the Size of the Illegal Migrant Population of Mexican Origin in the United States: An Assessment, Review and Proposal." In *Mexican Immigrants and Mexican Americans: An Evolving Relation.* H. Browning and R. de la Garza, eds. Austin: Center for Mexican American Studies, University of Texas, 1986: 13-36.

Bernardo, G. and E. Barajas. *Las Maquiladoras: Structural Adjustment and Regional Development.* Mexico: FFE/OEKO-México, 1987.

Bilateral Commission on the Future of the United States-Mexico Relations.*The Challenge of Interdependence: Mexico and the United States.* Lanham, MD: University Press of America, 1989.

Birdsall, N. "A Cost of Siblings: Child Schooling in Urban Colombia." *Research in Population Economics,* 2 (1980): 115-150.

Block,F. and R.Cloward. *The Mean Season: The Attack on the Welfare State.* New York: Pantheon Books, 1987.

"Borderland: 'A Third Nation.'" *U.S. News and World Report.* March, 1983: 39.

Borjas, G. *Friends or Strangers: The Impact of Immigrants on the U.S. Economy.* New York: Basic Books, 1990.

___. "Immigrants in the U.S. Labor Market: 1940-80." *American Economic Review,* 81 (2): 287-291.

Borjas, G. and M. Tienda. "The Economic Consequences of Immigration." *Science*, February 6, 1987: 645-651.

Bortz, J. "Problems and Prospects in the Mexican and Borderlands Economies." *Mexican Studies*, 7 (2): 303-318.

Boyd, A. Testimony before the U.S. House of Representatives Public Works Sub-Committee on Water Resources, March 11, 1988.

Brannon, J. and W. Lucker. "The Impact of Mexico's Economic Crisis on the Demographic Composition of the Maquiladora Labor Force." *Journal of Borderland Studies*, 4 (1): 39-70.

Briggs, V. *Immigration Policy and the American Labor Force*. Baltimore: Johns Hopkins University Press, 1985.

Briody, E. "Household Work/Subsistence Strategies Among Mexican Americans of the Lower Rio Grande Valley." Unpublished dissertation, University of Texas at Austin, 1985.

Bronars, S. "Immigration, Internal Migration, and Economic Growth, 1940-1980." Paper presented at the NBER Conference on the Determinants and Effects of Immigration on the U.S. and Source Economies, January 15-16, 1990.

Brook, K. "Patterns of Labor Force Participation in the U.S.- Mexico Border Region, 1970-1980." *Journal of Borderland Studies*, 1 (1): 109-132.

Browning, H. and R. de la Garza. eds. *Mexican Immigrants and Mexican Americans: An Evolving Relation*. Austin: Center for Mexican American Studies, University of Texas at Austin, 1986.

"Brownsville: Where the Port Sells the City." *Twin Plant News*, 6 (12): 57-60.

Bustamante, J. "Commodity Migrants: Structural Analysis of Mexican Immigration to the United States." In *Views Across the Border: The United States and Mexico*. S. Ross, ed. Albuquerque: University of New Mexico Press, 1978: 183-203.

___. "Measuring the Flow of Undocumented Immigrants." In *Measuring Migration to the United States: Origins, Consequences, and Policy Options*. Eds. W. Cornelius and J. Bustamante. San Diego: Center for U.S.- Mexican Studies, UC-San Diego, 1989: 95-108.

___. "Mexican Migration to the United States: De Facto Rules." In *Mexico and the United States: Studies in Economic Interaction*. ed. P. Musgrave. Boulder: Westview Press, 1985: 185-205.

Butcher, K. and D. Card. "Immigration and Wages: Evidence from the 1980's." *American Economic Review*, 81 (2): 292-296.

Calavita, K. "The Immigration Policy Debate: Critical Analysis and Future Options." In *Mexican Migration to the United States: Origins, Consequences, and Policy Options*. Ed. W. Cornelius and J. Bustamante. San Diego: Center for U.S.- Mexican Studies, UC-San Diego, 1989: 151-178.

___. *U.S. Immigration Law and the Control of Labor: 1820-1924*. San Diego: Academic Press, 1984.

Cassio, L. *The Economy of the Interdependency: Mexico and the US*. Mexico City: FCE, 1989.

Charboneau, E. Testimony before the U.S. House of Representatives Select Committee on Hunger, May 15, 1989.

Chrispin, B. "Employment and Manpower Development in the Maquiladora Industry: Reaching Maturity." In K. Fatemi, ed. *The Maquiladora Industry: Economic Solution or Problem?* New York: Praeger, 1990: 71-90.

Cobb, S. and D. Molina. "Implications of North American Free Trade for Infrastructure and Migration on the Texas-Mexico Border." In *North American Free Trade: Proceedings of a Conference.* Dallas, TX.: Federal Reserve Bank of Dallas, 1991, pp. 75-90.

Committee on Agriculture. U.S. House of Representatives. *Report to the Chairman: U.S. Mexico Trade.* Washington, DC: U.S. General Accounting Office, 1991.

Cornelius, W. "Mexican Migration to the United States: An Introduction." In *Mexican Migration to the United States: Origins, Consequences, and Policy Options.* Eds. W. Cornelius and J. Bustamante. San Diego: Center for U.S.- Mexican Studies, UC-San Diego, 1989: 1-24.

___. "The U.S. Demand for Mexican Labor." In *Mexican Migration to the United States: Origins, Consequences, and Policy Options.* Eds. W. Cornelius and J. Bustamante. San Diego: Center for U.S.- Mexican Studies, UC-San Diego, 1989:25-48.

Cornelius, W. and J. Bustamante, eds. *Mexican Migration to the United States: Origins, Consequences, and Policy Options.* San Diego: Center for U.S.- Mexican Studies, UC-San Diego, 1989.

Craig, R. *The Bracero Program: Interest Groups and Foreign Policy.* Austin: University of Texas Press, 1971.

Czinkota, M. ed. *U.S. - Latin American Trade Relations: Issues and Concerns.* New York: Praeger, 1983.

Danzinger, S., R. Haveman, and R. Plotnick. "How Income Transfers Affect Work, Savings, and the Income Distribution." *Journal of Economic Literature,* 99 (1981): 975-1028.

Department of Budget and Program Mission. *Mexican Census of Population.* Mexico City: INEGI, various years.

Díaz-Guerrero, R. "Mexicans and Americans: Two Worlds, One Border...and One Observer." In *Views Across the Border: The United States and Mexico.* Ed. S. Ross. Albuquerque: University of New Mexico Press, 1978: 283-307.

Dillman, C. "Assembly Industries in Mexico." *Journal of InterAmerican Studies and World Affairs.* (1981): 42-53.

___. "Urban Growth Along Mexico's Northern Border and the Mexican National Border Program." *Journal of Developing Areas,* 4 (1970): 487-508.

Dowty, A. *Closed Borders: The Contemporary Assault on Freedom of Movement.* New Haven: Yale University Press, 1987.

Eaton, D. and J. Anderson, eds. *The State of the Rio Grande-Rio Bravo: A Study of Water Resources Issues Along the Texas- Mexico Border.* Tucson: University of Arizona Press, 1987.

Eatwell, J., M. Milgate, and P. Newman, eds. *The New Palgrave Dictionary of Economics, Vol. 3.* New York: The Macmillan Press Ltd., 1987.

Echeverri-Carroll, E. "The Impact of a North American Free Trade Agreement on the Maquiladora Industry." In *North American Free Trade: Proceedings of a Conference.* Dallas, TX.: Federal Reserve Bank of Dallas, 1991, pp. 95-102.

Ehrenberg, R. and R. Smith. *Modern Labor Economics*. Glenview, IL: Scott, Foresman and Company, 1985.

Embassy of Mexico. *Mexico/United States Free Trade: Fact Sheets*. Washington, DC:
Office for Free Trade Agreement Negotiations, n.d.

English, W., S. Williams, and S. Ibarreche. "Employee Turnover in Maquiladoras."
Journal of Borderland Studies, 4 (2): 71-99.

Erb, R. and S. Ross, ed. *U.S. Policies Toward Mexico: Perceptions and Perspectives*.
Washington, DC: AEI, 1979.

___. *United States Relations with Mexico*. Washington, DC: AEI, 1981.

Ericson, A. "An Analysis of Mexico's Border Industrialization Program." *Monthly
Labor Review*, 93 (5): 33-40.

Ethier, W. "Illegal Immigration: The Host Country Problem." *American Economic
Review*, Vol. 76, No. 1 (March 1986): 56-71.

Evans, J. "Conditions of Employment and Income Distribution in Mexico." *IMR*,
13 (1): 4-24.

Fatemi, K., ed. *The Maquiladora Industry: Economic Solution or Problem?* New York:
Praeger, 1990.

Fehrenbach, T. *Texas: A Salute From Above*. San Antonio: World Publishing Services, Inc., 1985.

Fernández, J. and J. Tamayo. "Industry on the Northern Border of Mexico." In
Industrial Strategy and Planning in Mexico and the United States. Ed. S. Weintraub.
Boulder: Westview Press, 1986: 197-202.

Fernandez, R. "The Border Industrialization Program on the United States-Mexico
Border." *Review of Political Economy*, 5 (1): 37-52.

___. *The United States - Mexico Border*. Notre Dame: University of Notre Dame
Press, 1977.

___. *The Mexican-American Border Region*. Notre Dame: University of Notre Dame
Press, 1989.

Filer, R. "The Impact of Immigrant Arrivals on Migratory Patterns of Native Workers." Paper presented at the NBER Conference on the Determinants and Effects
of Immigration on the U.S. and Source Economies, January 15-16, 1990.

"Foreign and Mexican Capital of $10 Billion to Expand Mexico's Vibrant Tourism
Industry." *Wall Street Journal* (October 1, 1990): B12.

Fuentes, J. *Genesis of the American Expansionism*. Mexico City: ColMex, 1980.

Fuller, S. and C. Hall. "The U.S.- Mexico Free Trade Agreement: Issues and Implications for the U.S. and Texas Fresh Vegetable/Melon Industry." *Texas Agricultural Market Research Center, Research Report No. IM-2-91*. April 1991.

Galarza, E. *Merchants of Labor: The Mexican Bracero Story*. Charlotte, CA: McNally
and Loftin Publishers, 1964.

Galbraith, J. *The Nature of Mass Poverty*. Cambridge: Harvard University Press,
1977.

Gambrill, M. *Industrial Restructuration: Maquiladoras on the Mexico-U.S. Border*. Mexico City: CNFE, 1986.

___. *Maquiladoras: Patterns and Motives of Migration*. Mexico City: Ceesterm, 1981.

García, J. *Operation Wetback: The Mass Deportation of Mexican Undocumented Workers*.
Westport, CN: Greenwood Press, 1980.

George, E. "What Does the Future Hold for the Maquiladora Industry?" In K. Fatemi, ed. *The Maquiladora Industry: Economic Solution or Problem?* New York: Praeger, 1990: 219-234.

George, E. and W. Hoffman. "Growth Factors in the Maquila Industry." *Journal of Borderland Studies*, 6 (1): 87-98.

Gibney, F. Jr. "In Texas, a Grim New Appalachia." *Newsweek* (June 8, 1987): 27-28.

Gibson, L. and A. Renteria, eds. *The United States and Mexico: Borderland Development and the National Economies.* Boulder: Westview Press, 1985.

Ginneken, W. *Socio-Economic Groups and Income Distribution in Mexico.* New York: St. Martins Press, 1980.

Goodwin, Jr., H. "The U.S. - Mexico Free Trade Agreement: Agricultural Labor Issues." *Texas Agricultural Market Research Center, Research Report No. IM-11-91.* April 1991.

Greenwood, M. and J. McDowell. "The Factor Market Consequences of U.S. Immigration." *Journal of Economic Literature*, Vol. 24, No. 4 (December 1986): 1738-1772.

Gruben, W. "Mexican Maquiladora Growth: Does It Cost U.S. Jobs?" *Economic Review* (Jan. 1990): 15-29.

Hagenaars, A. and K. de Vos. "The Definition and Measurement of Poverty." *Journal of Human Resources*, 23 (2): 211-221.

Hansen, N. "Improving Economic Opportunity for the Mexican Americans." *Economic and Business Bulletin*, 22 (1969): 1-14.

___. *The Border Economy: Regional Development of the Southwest.* Austin: The University of Texas Press, 1981.

Harrington, M. *The Other America: Poverty in the United States.* New York: Penguin Books, 1981.

___. *The New American Poverty.* New York: Penguin Books, 1984.

Harwood, E. "American Public Opinion and U.S. Immigration Policy." *Annals of the American Academy of Political and Social Science*, Vol.487 (September 1986): 201-212.

Hayes, K., M. Nieswiadomy, and D. Slottje. "Multivariate Exogeneity Tests and Poverty." *Economic Letters*, 33 (1990): 395-399.

Holden, R. "Maquiladoras on the Texas/Mexico Border: An Econometric Evaluation of Employment and Retail Sales Effects on Four Texas SMSAs." Master's Professional Report, LBJ School of Public Affairs, University of Texas at Austin, 1984.

House, J. *Frontier on the Rio Grande: A Political Geography of Development and Social Deprivation.* Oxford: Clarendon Press, 1982.

Hufbauer, G. and J. Schott. *NAFTA: An Assessment.* Washington, DC: Institute for International Economics, 1993.

___. *North American Free Trade: Issues and Recommendations.* Washington, DC: Institute for International Economics, 1992.

Hunter, L. "U.S. Trade Protection: Effects on the Industrial and Regional Composition of Employment." *Economic Review* (Jan. 1990): 1-13.

International Monetary Fund. *IMF Government Finance Statistics.* Washington, DC: International Monetary Fund, various years.

Institute of Economic Research. *The Commercial Integration of Mexico to the U.S. and Canada.* Mexico City: UNAM-XXI Century, 1990.

Institutional Investor. *1990 Pensions Directory*. New York: Harper & Row, 1990.

Jones, K. Testimony before the U.S. House of Representatives Select Committee on Public Works and Transportation, March 12, 1988.

Jones. L., T. Ozuna, Jr., and M. Wright. "The U.S.- Mexico Free Trade Agreement: Economic Impacts on the Border Region." *Texas Agricultural Market Research Center, Research Report No. IM-16-91*. June 1991.

Jones, R. *Explaining Origin Patterns of Undocumented Migration to South Texas in Recent Years*. Boulder: Westview Press, 1984.

Juhn, C., K. Murphy, and B. Pierce. "Wage Inequality and the Rise in the Return to Skill." *Journal of Political Economy* (forthcoming).

Katz, L., G. Borjas, and R. Freeman. "On the Labor Market Effects of Immigration and Trade." Paper presented at the NBER Conference on the Determinants and Effects of Immigration on the U.S. and Source Economies, January 15-16, 1990.

Klein, E. "Made in Mexico." *D&B Reports* (Jan.- Feb, 1991): 26-61.

Kramer, M. "Life on the Line: the U.S.- Mexican Border." *National Geographic* (June 1985): 720-749.

LaLonde, R. and R. Topel. "Immigrants in the American Labor Market: Quality, Assimilation, and Distributional Effects." *American Economic Review*, 81 (2): 297-302.

Langham, T. "Federal Regulation of Border Labor: Operation Wetback and the Wetback Bill." *Journal of Borderland Studies*, 7 (1): 81-91.

Larson, C. *Headin' South: The Texas Snowbirds*. Austin: Hogg Foundation for Mental Health, 1986.

LBJ School of Public Affairs. *Colonias in the Lower Rio Grande Valley of South Texas: A Summary Report*. Austin: The University of Texas, Policy Research Project No. 18, 1977.

Leamer, E. "Wage Effects of a U.S.- Mexican Free Trade Agreement." Paper presented at the Mexico-U.S. FTA Conference, Brown University, October, 1991.

Lee, S. "From Valley to New Peaks?" *The Dallas Morning News*. (Monday, January 4, 1993): 1D.

Levy, D. and G. Szekely. *Mexico: Paradoxes of Stability and Change*. Boulder, CO: Westview Press, 1983.

Lipton, M. *Why Poor People Stay Poor*. Cambridge: Harvard University Press, 1977.

"Looking Ahead to the Future." *The Bulletin of First City Development Services Group*, 2 (1): 1-4.

Loe, V. "Beyond City Limits." *The Dallas Morning News*. (Sunday, February 28, 1993): 22-23.

Madsen, W. *The Mexican-Americans of South Texas*. New York: Holt, Reinhart and Winston, 1964.

Maril, R. *Poorest of Americans*. Notre Dame: University of Notre Dame Press, 1989.

Marquez, S. "Presidential Promises: What Will Clinton Do For Hispanics?" *Hispanic* (Jan./Feb. 1993): 23-28.

Martinez, M. Testimony to the U.S. House of Representatives Select Committee on Public Works and Transportation, March, 12, 1988.

McCarthy, K. and R. Valdez. *Current and Future Effects of Mexican Immigration in California*. Santa Monica, CA: Rand Corporation, 1986.

McGreevey, W. *Third World Poverty*. Lexington, MA: Lexington Books, 1980.

Meissner, F. "In-bond Industries as Development Tools." *Third World Quarterly*. (1979): 141-147.

___. "Mexican Border and Free Zone Areas: Implications for Development." In *U.S.- Latin American Trade Relations: Issues and Concerns*. Ed. M. Czinkota. New York: Praeger, 1983: 253-278.

Mexican Economic Outlook. Philadelphia: Ciemex-Wefa, 1991.

Mexican Foreign Investment. Mexico City: Secofin, 1990.

Mexico-U.S. Fact Sheets. Washington, DC: Embassy of Mexico, 1990.

"Mexico's Poverty: Driving Force for Border Jumpers." *U.S. News and World Report* (March, 1983): 42-43.

Michie, D. "Implications of a North American Free Trade Agreement for the Border." In *North American Free Trade: Proceedings of a Conference*. Dallas, TX: 1991, pp. 91-94.

Miller, M. *Economic Growth and Change along the U.S. - Mexican Border*. Austin: Bureau of Business Research, 1982.

Miller, M. and R. Maril. *Poverty in the Lower Rio Grande Valley of Texas*. College Station: Texas Agricultural Experiment Station, Texas A&M University, 1978.

Molina, D. and S. Cobb. "The Impact of Maquiladora Investment on the Size Distribution of Income Along the U.S.- Mexico Border: The Case of Texas." *Journal of Borderland Studies*, 4 (2): 100-118.

Moore, J. *Mexican-Americans*. Englewood Cliffs, NJ: Printice Hall, 1976.

Musgrave, P. ed. *Mexico and the United States: Studies in Economic Interaction*. Boulder: Westview Press, 1985.

Myers, J. *The Border Wardens*. Englewood Cliffs, NJ: Prentice-Hall, 1971.

Nash, J. and K. Fernandez. *Women, Men and the International Division of Labor*. Albany, NY: State University of New York, 1983.

National Bank of Mexico. *Economic Statistics*. Mexico City: Banamex, various years.

National Center for Health Statistics. *Vital Statistics of the U.S.* Hyattsville, MD: U.S. Department of Health and Human Services, various years.

National Council of Population. *A Survey on the Northern Mexican Border of Undocumented Workers Returned by U.S. Officials: Report of Statistical Results*. Mexico City: CONAPO-SG, 1986.

Nibbe, D. "Maquila Locations in the Interior." *Twin Plant News*, 5 (10): 27-29.

___. "McAllen/Reynosa." *Twin Plant News*, 3 (10): 12-17.

North American Free Trade: Proceedings of a Conference. Dallas, TX: Federal Reserve Bank of Dallas, 1991.

"Number of People Receiving Food Stamps Hits Record High." *The Dallas Morning News*. (Tuesday, March 2, 1993): 3.

Office of Strategic Management, Research, and Development. *The Colonias Factbook: A Survey of Living Conditions in Rural Areas of South Texas and West Texas Border Counties*. Austin, TX: Texas Department of Human Services, 1988.

Osberg, L. ed. *Economic Inequality and Poverty: International Perspectives*. Armonk, NY: M.E. Sharpe, 1991.

Papke, L. "Tax Policy and Urban Development: Evidence from an Enterprise Zone Program." NBER Working Paper No. 3945. Cambridge: National Bureau of

Economic Research, 1992.

Patrick, J. "The Employment Impact of Maquiladoras Along the U.S. Border." In K. Fatemi, ed. *The Maquiladora Industry: Economic Solution or Problem?* New York: Praeger, 1990: 57-70.

___. "Maquiladoras and South Texas Border Economic Development." *Journal of Borderland Studies,* 4 (1): 89-98.

___. "Study Identifies Opportunities for Suppliers of Maquiladoras." *Twin Plant News,* 4 (5): 24-25.

Pellicer, O. *The Politics of the United States and Mexico.* Mexico City: ColMex, 1979.

Pierce, F. *A Brief History of the Lower Rio Grande Valley.* Wisconsin: George Santa Publishing Company, 1917.

Pluta, J., ed. *Economic and Business Issues of the 1980s.* Austin: Bureau of Business Research, UTA, 1980.

President's Council of Economic Advisors. *Economic Report to the President.* Washington, DC: U.S. Government Printing Office, 1991.

Reisler, M. *By the Sweat of Their Brow: Mexican Immigrant Labor in the United States, 1900-1940.* Westport, CN: Greenwood Press, 1976.

"Relief from Illegals? Perhaps in 50 Years." *U.S. News and World Report* (March, 1983): 44.

"Resurgence in illegal immigration expected to continue." *The Dallas Morning News* (Weds., Dec. 18, 1991): 38A.

Resources, Community, and Economic Development Division. *Rural Development: Problems and Progress of Colonia Subdivisions Near Mexico Border.* Washington, DC: U.S. General Accounting Office, 1990.

Review of Trade and Investment Liberalization Measures by Mexico and Prospects for Future United States-Mexico Relations. Washington, DC: United States International Trade Commission, 1990.

Reyes, L. *The Maquiladora Industry in Reynosa, Tamaulipas: Socio-Economic Aspects.* Monterey, N.L.: UANL, 1988.

Reynolds, C. "Mexican-U.S. Interdependence: Economic and Social Perspectives." In *U.S. - Mexico Relations: Economic and Social Aspects.* Eds. C. Reynolds and C. Tello. Stanford: Stanford University Press, 1983: 21-45.

Reynolds, C. and C. Tello, eds. *U.S.- Mexico Relations: Economic and Social Aspects.* Stanford: Stanford University Press, 1983.

Rich, J. "Environmental Protection: A New Trade Issue." In *North American Free Trade: Proceedings of a Conference.* Dallas, TX: Federal Reserve Bank of Dallas, 1991, pp. 67-74.

Rivera-Batiz, F. "Can Border Industries Be a Substitute for Immigration?" *American Economic Review,* 76 (2): 263-268.

Ross, S., ed. *Views Across the Border: The United States and Mexico.* Albuquerque: University of New Mexico Press, 1978.

Rosson, III, C. and F. Adcock. "The U.S.- Mexico Free Trade Agreement: Issues and Implications for the U.S. and Texas Citrus Industry." *Texas Agricultural Market Research Center, Research Report No. IM-3-91.* April 1991.

Rosson, III, C., B. Schulthies, and D. White. "The U.S.- Mexico Free Trade Agreement: Issues and Implications for the U.S. and Texas Livestock and Meat Industry." *Texas Agricultural Market Research Center, Research Report No. IM-5-91.* April 1991.

Rush, C. Jr. "Winter Texans in the Lower Rio Grande Valley." In *Economic and Business Issues of the 1980s.* Ed. J. Pluta. Austin: Bureau of Business Research, 1980.

Salinas, E. Testimony before the U.S. House of Representatives Select Committee on Hunger, May 15, 1989.

Sanchez, R. "Environment: Mexican Perspective." In *U.S.- Mexican Industrial Integration: The Road to Free Trade.* Ed. S. Weintraub. Boulder: Westview Press, 1990.

Sanderson, S. "Automated Manufacturing and Offshore Assembly in Mexico." In *The United States and Mexico: Face to Face with New Technology,* ed. C. Thorup. New York: Transaction Books, 1987: pp. 127-148.

Sawhill, I. "Poverty in the U.S.: Why Is It So Persistent?" *Journal of Economic Literature,* 26 (1988): 1073-1119.

Scheinman, M. "Report on the Present Status of Maquiladora." In K. Fatemi, ed. *The Maquiladora Industry: Economic Solution or Problem?* New York: Praeger, 1990: 19-36.

Schoenberger, E. "Technological and Organizational Change in Automobile Production: Spatial Implications." *Regional Studies,* Vol. 21, No. 3: 199-214.

Schulthies, B. and R. Schwart. "The U.S.- Mexico Free Trade Agreement: Issues and Implications for the U.S. and Texas Dairy Industry." *Texas Agricultural Market Research Center, Research Report No. IM-10-91.* August 1991.

Schulthies, B. and G. Williams. "U.S.- Mexico Agricultural Trade and Mexican Agriculture: Linkages and Prospects Under a Free Trade Agreement." *Texas Agricultural Market Research Center, Research Report No. IM-6-92.* July 1992.

Seligson, M. and E. Williams. *Maquiladoras and Migration Workers in the Mexico - United States Border Industrialization Program.* Austin: Mexico-United States Border Research Program, 1981.

Sinson. J. "Maquiladoras Challenge Human Resources." *Personnel Journal* (Nov. 1989): 90-93.

Stambaugh, J and L. Stambaugh. *The Lower Rio Grande Valley of Texas: Its Colonization and Industrialization, 1518-1953.* Austin: San Felipe Press, 1964.

Statistical Agenda of Mexico. Mexico City: INEGI.SPP, various years.

Statistics of the Maquiladora Industry of Exportation. Mexico City: INEGI, 1991.

Stoddard, E. *Borderlands Sourcebook. A Guide to the Literature on Northern Mexico and the American Southwest.* Norman: University of Oklahoma Press, 1983.

___. *Maquila: Assembly Plants in Northern Mexico.* El Paso: Texas Western Press, 1987.

Stoddard, E. and J. Hedderson. *Trends and Patterns of Poverty Along the U.S.- Mexico Border.* Borderland Research Monograph Series No. 3. El Paso: Organization of U.S. Border Cities and Counties, University of Texas at El Paso, 1987.

Stolp, C. and J. Hockenyos. "Texas Under Free Trade: Some Sectoral, Regional, and Modeling Considerations." In *North American Free Trade: Proceedings of a Conference.* Dallas, TX: Federal Reserve Bank of Dallas, 1991: 53-66.

Survey of Undocumented Mexican Workers Returned from the U.S. Report of Statis-

tical Results. Mexico City: CONAPO-SG, 1986.

Taylor, M. "The U.S.- Mexico Free Trade Agreement: Issues and Implications for the U.S. and Texas Cotton Industry." *Texas Agricultural Market Research Center, Research Report No. IM-6-91.* April 1991.

Taylor, P. "Mexican Labor in the U.S." In University of California, *Publications in Economics, Vol. 6, 7, and 12.* Berkeley: University of California Press, 1930-1934.

___. "Migratory Farm Labor in the U.S." *Monthly Labor Review,* 44 (3): 537-549.

Texas Senate Committee on Natural Resources. *Interim Report to the 70th Legislature,* January, 1987.

Teutli, G. "The Maquiladora Industry: Foreign Exchange Earning and Employment." *Mexican Economist* (1978): 1073-1189.

Texas Department of Commerce. *Texas and the U.S.- Mexico Free Trade Agreement.* Austin: Office of Trade Development, 1991.

The Dallas Morning News. *Texas Almanac.* Houston: Gulf Publishing, various years.

The Impact of Mexican Trade on the Texas Economy: An Analysis of Current Patterns and Some Potential Effects of a Free Trade Agreement. Waco, TX: Perryman Consultants, 1991.

Thorup. C. ed. *The United States and Mexico: Fact to Face with Technology.* New York: Transaction Books, 1987.

Thurston, C. "Proposed Accord Fuels Expansion of US-Mexican Road, Rail Links." *The Journal of Commerce* (July 8, 1990): 1A and 10A.

Tienda, M. "Looking to the 1990s: Mexican Immigration in Sociological Perspective." In *Measuring Migration to the United States: Origins, Consequences, and Policy Options.* Eds. W. Cornelius and J. Bustamante. San Diego: Center for U.S.- Mexican Studies, 1989.

Trotter, R. "Cultural Barriers to the Delivery of Health Care to Mexican Americans in the Lower Rio Grande Valley of Texas." Unpublished dissertation, Southern Methodist University, 1976.

Tullock, G. *The Economics of Wealth and Poverty.* Boston: Kluwer, 1986.

Tyson, L. and J. Zysman. *The Dynamics of Trade and Employment.* Cambridge: Harper & Row, 1988.

United States International Trade Commission. *Review of Trade and Investment Liberalization Measures by Mexico and Prospects for Future United States - Mexican Relations.* Washington, D.C.: USITC, 1990.

___. *The Likely Impact on the United States of a Free Trade Agreement with Mexico.* Washington, D.C.: USITC, 1990.

Urquidi, V. and S. Villarreal. "Economic Importance of Mexico's Northern Border Region." In Ross, S. ed. *Views Across the Border: The United States and Mexico.* Albuquerque: University of New Mexico Press, 1978.

U.S. Congress. "Omnibus Trade and Competitiveness Act of 1988." In *Congressional Record.* Washington, DC: U.S. Government Printing Office, 1988.

U.S. Congress. House Committee on Public Works and Transportation. "Hearings before the Subcommittee on Water Resources, Inadequate Water Supply, and Sewage Disposal Facilities Associated With Colonias Along the United States - Mexico Border, No. 100-50, 100th Congress, 2nd Session." (March 11, 1988 at El

Paso, TX and March 12, 1988 at Brownsville, TX).

U.S. Department of Commerce, Bureau of the Census. *Characteristics of the Poor. Current Population Reports, Series P-60, no. 106*. Washington, DC: U.S. Government Printing Office, 1990.

___. *County Business Patterns 1988*. Washington, DC: U.S. Government Printing Office, 1990.

___. *Historical Statistics of the United States: Colonial Times to the Present*. Washington, DC: U.S. Government Printing Office, 1975.

___. *U.S. Population Census*. Washington, DC: U.S. Government Printing Office, various years.

___. *Statistical Abstract of the United States*. Washington, DC: U.S. Government Printing Office, various years.

U.S. Department of Justice, Immigration, and Naturalization Service. *Statistical Yearbook of the Immigration and Naturalization Service*. Washington, DC: Government Printing Office, various years.

U.S. Department of Labor. *Handbook of Labor Statistics, Bulletin 2340*. Washington, DC: U.S. Government Printing Office, 1991.

Vazquez, J. and L. Meyer. *Mexico's Face to the United States: A Historical Essay 1976-1988*. Mexico City: FCE, 1989.

Verea, C. *United States: Society, Culture and Education*. México: UNAM, 1991.

Vernez, G. and D. Ronfeldt. "The Current Situation in Mexican Immigration." *Science*, Vol. 251 (March 8, 1991): 1189-1193.

Vernon, R. *The Dilemma of Mexico's Development*. Cambridge: Harvard University Press, 1963.

Waller, M., G. Williams, and D. White. "The U.S.- Mexico Free Trade Agreement: Issues and Implications for the U.S. and Texas Grain and Feeds Industry." *Texas Agricultural Market Research Center, Research Report No. IM-4-91*. April 1991.

Weintraub. S. ed. *Industrial Strategy and Planning in Mexico and the United States*. Boulder: Westview Press, 1986.

Weintraub, S. "Illegal Immigrants in Texas: Impact on Social Services and Related Considerations." *International Migration Review*, Vol. 18, No. 3 (Fall 1984): 733-747.

___. *A Marriage of Convenience: Relations Between Mexico and the United States*. New York: Oxford University Press, 1990.

Weintraub, S., et al. "Preliminary Results: The Impact of a Free Trade Agreement with Mexico on Texas." In *North American Free Trade: Proceedings of a Conference*. Dallas, TX.: Federal Reserve Bank of Dallas, 1991. pp. 45-52.

Weintraub, S. ed. *U.S.- Mexican Industrial Integration: The Road to Free Trade*. Boulder: Westview Press, 1990.

Weintraub, S. and L. Boske. *U.S.- Mexico Free Trade Agreement: Economic Impact on Texas*. Austin: LBJ School of Public Policy, 1992.

Williams, E. "Attitudes and Strategies Inhibiting the Unionization of the Maquiladora Industry: Government, Industry, Unions, and Workers." *Journal of Borderland Studies*, 6 (2): 51-72.

Williams, G. and C. Rosson,III. "The U.S.- Mexico Free Trade Agreement: Issues and Implications for U.S. and Texas Agriculture." *Texas Agricultural Market Research Center, Research Report No. IM-1-91*. April 1991.

Williams, G. and B. Schulthies. "Agricultural Labor Effects of a U.S.- Mexico Free Trade Agreement: A U.S. Perspective." *Texas Agricultural Market Research Center, Research Report No. IM-4-92*. June 1992.

Williamson, R. *The Lower Rio Grande Valley of Texas*. Austin: Bureau of Business Research, 1965.

Wilson, P. *Exports and Local Development: Mexico's New Maquiladoras*. Austin: University of Texas Press, 1992.

___. "The Global Assembly Industry: Maquiladoras in International Perspective." *Journal of Borderland Studies*, 6 (2): 73-104.

World Bank. *World Development Report*. New York: Oxford University Press, various years.

Wright, R., et al. *The Texas Fact Book*. Austin: Bureau of Business Research, various years.

Zlatkovich, C. *Texas Metropolitan Area Profiles*. Austin: Bureau of Business Research, 1980.

About the Book and Author

With the North American Free Trade Agreement (NAFTA) looming large and imminent, the authors of this book explore the socio-economic fabric of the U.S.-Mexico border region as a measure of NAFTA's future. *Crisis on the Rio Grande* presents the social and economic history, as well as the potential, of the Lower Rio Grande Valley on the Texas-Mexico border. The authors discuss issues of poverty, *colonias*, the maquiladora industry, border migration, and NAFTA's potential impact on the economy, infrastructure, and environment of the border region. This timely study will interest economists, policy analysts, U.S.-Mexico border region specialists, and students of the North American Free Trade Agreement.

Dianne C. Betts is adjunct assistant professor of economics and history at Southern Methodist University. **Daniel J. Slottje** is associate professor of economics at Southern Methodist University.

Index